# THE FOOD DOCTOR EVERYDAY DIET

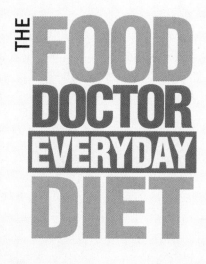

# THE FOOD DOCTOR EVERYDAY DIET

## Ian Marber Dip ION

Keep in touch and stay in shape
Sign up at **www.dk.com/fooddoctortips** to receive
a monthly email full of encouragement from
Ian Marber, The Food Doctor

For more information on The Food Doctor,
visit **www.thefooddoctor.com**

LONDON, NEW YORK, MELBOURNE,
MUNICH AND DELHI

For my wonderful mother
with thanks, appreciation and love

With special thanks to Rowena Paxton for her
truly delicious recipes and to George, Alistair and
Henrietta Paxton for being willing guinea pigs

**Project Editors** Jennifer Lane, Janice Anderson
**Project Designer** Jo Grey
**Senior Art Editor** Rosamund Saunders
**Managing Editor** Stephanie Farrow
**Publishing Manager** Gillian Roberts
**DTP designer** Sonia Charbonnier
**Production Controller** Stuart Masheter
**Art Director** Carole Ash
**Publishing Director** Mary-Clare Jerram
**Food stylist and home economist** Pippin Britz
**Photographer** Sian Irvine

First published in Great Britain in 2004 by
Dorling Kindersley Limited,
80 Strand, London WC2R 0RL

A Penguin Company

2 4 6 8 10 9 7 5 3

Copyright © 2005 Dorling Kindersley Limited, London
Text copyright © 2005 Ian Marber

**Always consult your health practitioner before starting a
nutrition programme if you have any health concerns.**

A CIP catalogue record for
this book is available from
the British Library

ISBN 1 4053 0605 X

Colour reproduced by
Colourscan, Singapore
Printed and bound in Portugal by
Printer Portuguesa

Discover more at
**www.dk.com**

# Contents

# Everyday eating

# Introduction

My aim in writing *The Food Doctor Everyday Diet* is to show you how easy it can be to lose weight at a sustainable rate, while eating nutritious food and not having to cut out any food groups.

The Food Doctor plan was written after many thousands of hours of working with people who wanted to lose weight. The principles that I believe in are safe, accessible, and easy to incorporate into any lifestyle. I know they work and have witnessed their success time and time again. There are no potentially unhealthy side-effects and they re-establish the value of proper food in the complicated arena of weight management. The 10 principles (*see pp.12–13*) that form the foundation of my plan are very simple to incorporate into your everyday life, yet so effective.

### A diet for the real world

So, what is The Food Doctor Everyday Diet? Simply that. A diet you can follow every day without actually feeling as though you're "on a diet" at all: a diet that can work for you whatever your lifestyle. Over a number of years, I have gathered feedback from private clients ranging from us regular folk to musicians, actors, performers and models. Each situation was different, and so my diet plan evolved to suit all situations and life-styles, including work, staying home and a multitude of careers and life pressures. Whether you're single or married, male or female, childless or child-laden, this diet is easy to incorporate into your everyday life.

Many of you will have previously been on very prescriptive diets, i.e. those that demand that you eat a specific food in a specific amount. With my diet, it's up to you: the recipes work best with the listed foods, but if you don't like something, then by all means substitute one protein for another, or one complex carbohydrate for another. It's your choice, and it's not magic – just sensible, balanced, non-faddy eating in a way that will encourage safe weight loss without side-effects.

In this book you will find more than 100 delicious recipes that are all diet-friendly (although many could be served up at a dinner party without your guests ever guessing that they were eating "your diet" with you). They can be mixed and matched as you choose – I've made some

What is **The Food Doctor** plan?
It is based on "fuelling up" frequently with
an ideal combination of **protein** and
**complex carbohydrates** at every meal

If you get to a **point** where you **see food** simply as something that will make you **fat or thin**, then **your vision** has become blurred

suggestions, but I hope you will also explore the options for yourself. There are menu ideas to show you how easy it is to combine the food groups according to The Food Doctor plan, and suggestions for how to "tweak" common meal choices to make them that much healthier.

Often this tweaking involves taking into account the glycaemic index (GI) rating of foods. This is a key factor in The Food Doctor plan, which is geared to fuelling your body with a steady flow of energy and minimising the production of insulin. This is one diet that *doesn't* want you to skip any meals! We examine how food is converted into glucose and the importance of eating in a way that regulates the speed at which that conversion occurs – too rapidly or too slowly will confuse your metabolism and potentially lead to even more weight gain when you return to your "normal" eating patterns.

"I have been on the diet and can honestly say I haven't looked back! I have lost 56lbs, I feel marvellous and very proud of myself. I have never before been on a diet where I have never felt hungry but this is it!"

Sharon Clifton, SOUTHEND-ON-SEA

### Time for change

The plan is designed to be practical for those of us that live in the "real world", not in a world of denial, weighing food, starving or bingeing. One reader described my earlier book, *The Food Doctor Diet*, as "A food plan for grown ups" and, while it works for children too, I really relate to that idea. Time seems to be a huge barrier to sensible eating for many people, but with The Food Doctor plan healthy eating becomes a quick, simple option: many of the meal ideas take only minutes to prepare and can actually be quicker than waiting for the microwave to go "ping" with your bought ready-made meal. Time – and how to make the most of it – is a key element of *The Food Doctor Everyday Diet.*

Since I published *The Food Doctor Diet* in 2004, many readers have written to tell me how well it has worked for them. With questions from readers, I have been able to develop the plan and explore new ways of explaining it more clearly for you. This book is the result of that process – a development that expands on the 10 principles outlined in the first book and provides you with even more inspirational ideas on how to incorporate them smoothly and simply into your life. And it doesn't stop here: log on to www.dk.com/fooddoctortips and I'll keep you up-to-date on my latest thoughts and ideas.

One of my key messages concerns how food seems to have become devalued. This is a major factor in why many people have gained weight in the first place, and it's time to revisit the important basics of food. We need re-educating on how to eat, and in turn need to educate children about better eating habits, so that excess weight is not something we pass on to the next generation. The health risks associated with obesity are yet to be really felt and health services worldwide will be further stretched than ever. All because of the food that we eat.

"I did the diet and lost 6lbs, just the boost I needed. I am now trying to stick to the principles and have loads more energy than I used to have. My husband has joined me in trying to eat more healthily and even the children are enjoying the food. It is so refreshing to have an easy diet to stick to."

Sue Oliver, SOMERSET

## Fads and fashions

Every year there are a plethora of new diet books making claims for instant weight loss. But why are there new diet books every year when nothing has changed in the world of cells in millions of years? The only thing that has changed is the food we eat, along with a food industry hungry for profits and the lack of priority we are now attaching to food. We are all hoping for an easy way to lose weight – something cutting-edge yet easy to do, inexpensive and instant.

But the truth is that there isn't anything new. The body breaks down food in exactly the same way it did when we were living in caves, and no new food has been invented for some time (aside from processed food!) so it seems obvious to me why fad diets cannot work. The problem is that the cutting-edge, well-marketed diet is still a diet, with a beginning, a middle and an end, and so you will "be good", "come off it" or "cheat" and so the cycle begins again.

The Food Doctor plan is one for life, not the short term, and once you understand the principles and incorporate them into your life, you will find that it makes for an easier life, together with true weight loss.

The **Food Doctor** plan aims to provide you with a **steady flow** of **energy** – this is one diet that **doesn't** want you to **skip meals**

# Principles and science

The 10 Food Doctor principles, my essential guidelines on how to eat, are based on some fascinating concepts. This chapter will show you how poor food choices and long-term or crash dieting can affect your insulin levels and metabolic rate. You can then, more importantly, discover why The Food Doctor Everyday Diet is the answer.

# The 10 principles

These principles are key to my way of eating. They are the "building blocks" for the Everyday Diet and have been designed to be simple to remember and straightforward to incorporate into your lifestyle. There are no complicated calorie-counting or points systems. Sticking to the 10 principles is easy and will give you the tools to control your weight, feel healthier and have a better attitude to food.

## PRINCIPLE 1

### Eat protein with complex carbohydrates

Combining these food groups in the correct proportions will ensure that you receive a steady flow of energy, as the body converts foods relatively slowly into glucose. You can then avoid triggering insulin production, therefore minimising the potential for your body to store food as fat (*see pp.14–19*).

## PRINCIPLE 2

### Stay hydrated

It is important to drink plenty of water, preferably at least 1.5 litres (3½ pints) a day, and even more during hot weather or if you are exercising. Remember that, by the time your body tells you that you are thirsty, you are already dehydrated. Limiting your alcohol and salt intake is important too, as these dehydrate the body.

## PRINCIPLE 3

### Eat a wide variety of food

It is easy to get stuck in a routine when shopping: in fact, for 90 per cent of the time the majority of us buy just 10 per cent of the variety of foods that are actually available to us. Try introducing two new foods to your shopping trolley every week.

## PRINCIPLE 4

### Fuel up frequently

Eating the right foods little and often is a vital part of The Food Doctor plan. Doing this gives you a constant supply of energy throughout the day, avoiding the insulin rollercoaster (*see pp.16–17*) and making hunger, tiredness and food cravings a feature of the past.

PRINCIPLE 5

## Eat breakfast

Breakfast is essential: eating a balanced breakfast supplies you with the fuel to help maintain energy levels and set your metabolism up for the day. It can be hard to fit it into a busy lifestyle, but taking a few minutes to eat breakfast is fundamental to controlling your weight in the long term.

PRINCIPLE 6

## Avoid sugar

Sugar is present in food in many different forms (*see p.20*), all of which break down into glucose extremely quickly and all of which therefore contribute to fat production and weight gain. The speed at which sugar converts to blood glucose creates a high, and the resulting low causes hunger.

PRINCIPLE 7

## Exercise is essential

Making progress with The Food Doctor plan does not just depend on changing your attitude towards food. Exercise and healthy eating need to go hand-in-hand in order to get results. However busy your everyday schedule, aim to fit in 30 minutes of exercise three times a week.

PRINCIPLE 8

## Follow the 80:20 rule

It is perfectly normal to "stray" every now and then. If you follow The Food Doctor Diet for at least 80 per cent of the time, then you can stray for 20 per cent of the time. This means you can enjoy social occasions without feeling guilty, and also escape the boredom and frustration associated with other diet regimes.

PRINCIPLE 9

## Make time to eat

Eating has become rather devalued today. Often it is crammed between more "important" events, and we barely have time to sit down to enjoy our food. Taking time out for a meal is far more beneficial to digestive health, as well as being more satisfying.

PRINCIPLE 10

## Eat fat to lose fat

If you are used to counting calories, you probably view fat as the enemy. However, there are certain essential fats (omega-3 and omega-6) that the body needs to function properly. The key is to eat less saturated fat and to ensure that you consume enough of the essential fats.

# The GI factor

You've probably heard of expressions such as "sugar cravings", "energy slumps", "sugar highs" and "high GI". These relate to the rollercoaster ride of insulin production that many of us put our bodies through by making mistakes in our food choices and dietary habits.

The food you eat is turned by the body into glucose, which is its source of fuel for creating energy. Glucose levels in the body are constantly monitored and kept within strict boundaries by hormones that store glucose away when there's too much of it in the blood and release it again when levels are low.

### Insulin and the GI index

Glucose is stored short-term as glycogen in the muscles and liver, but if glucose levels become high and glycogen stores are full, a hormone called insulin is released to store the excess glucose as fat until the body needs to convert it back to glucose for energy (*see opposite*).

This can have a rollercoaster effect on the body (*see pp.16–17*). In terms of weight loss and gain, it means that, if we eat the sort of foods that raise the body's glucose levels too high, or that encourage the body to release too much glucose, then glucose storage speeds up. Since the job of insulin is effectively to encourage the storage of excess glucose, clearly we need to limit the amount of insulin that the body creates in order to discourage the storage of fat. The trick is to choose foods that break down slowly into glucose and therefore avoid

triggering insulin production. However, we should also eat in a manner that does not allow insulin levels to fall too low, since that in turn can also cause serious health problems. Knowing which foods are high in sugar and which ones trigger insulin production is essential to understanding how The Food Doctor plan works. It is why one of my 10 principles advocates fuelling up frequently and why I recommend eating foods with low scores on the glycaemic index (GI).

A food's GI score is based upon how quickly it converts to glucose in the body. Foods with a high score convert rapidly into glucose (and therefore trigger insulin production), while foods with low scores convert more slowly and are therefore unlikely to raise blood-glucose levels above the insulin threshold.

### What influences insulin production?

A number of foods and other factors have a rapid effect on insulin production, while other foods and factors have very little effect. Watching out for these "highs" and "lows" is key to my plan, but it's very easy to remember and incorporate into your everyday life. The five main "highs" that raise glucose levels and trigger insulin production, and therefore fat storage, are sugar, simple carbohydrates, stress, smoking and caffeine (*see pp.20–23*). These are the factors to avoid.

So what are the "lows" that help you maintain steady blood-glucose levels, keeping insulin production at bay and therefore avoiding fat storage in the body?

**Protein** This is quite hard for the body to break down. In other words, it takes longer for the glucose to be extracted, which keeps blood-glucose levels even.

**Complex carbohydrates** Unlike simple carbohydrates, complex carbohydrates are fibre-dense, so it takes longer for the body to break them down into glucose than it does for it to break down simple carbohydrates.

---

### HOW IS INSULIN LINKED TO FAT?

Minimising insulin production in the body is an important factor in The Food Doctor plan. To understand why this is, you need to be aware of the relevance of two of its functions in relation to potential weight loss:

● Insulin is a catalyst for the creation of new fat

● Insulin inhibits the breakdown of fat

continued p.18

# How food can turn into fat

The food you eat is broken down into glucose and transported to every cell in your body via the bloodstream to provide fuel (*see right*). If this process takes place too rapidly, or if you eat especially large amounts of food, then the levels of glucose created will be surplus to requirements. This surplus has to go somewhere, so it is stored in a base of water known as glycogen, held in the muscles and liver. Glycogen stores have a limit to what they can hold and, when they are full, the excess is stored away as fat (*see below*).

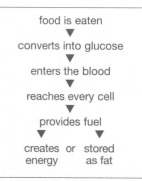

food is eaten
▼
converts into glucose
▼
enters the blood
▼
reaches every cell
▼
provides fuel
▼          ▼
creates  or  stored
energy      as fat

**Food converts to glucose**
Food enters the body and is converted into blood-glucose to provide energy.

**Short-term storage**
If the immediate energy requirements are not high enough to use all the available glucose, or if glucose enters the system too rapidly, any overflow is stored short-term in the liver and muscles in a base of water known as glycogen.

**Excess glucose becomes fat**
If the body's stores of glycogen reach their limit, the overflow of excess glucose still available is stored as fat.

# THE INSULIN ROLLERCOASTER

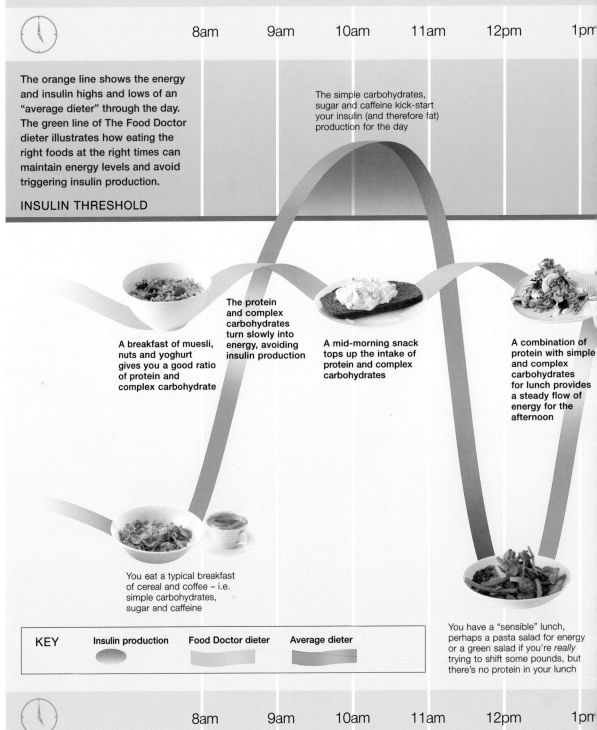

8am    9am    10am    11am    12pm    1pm

The orange line shows the energy and insulin highs and lows of an "average dieter" through the day. The green line of The Food Doctor dieter illustrates how eating the right foods at the right times can maintain energy levels and avoid triggering insulin production.

INSULIN THRESHOLD

The simple carbohydrates, sugar and caffeine kick-start your insulin (and therefore fat) production for the day

The protein and complex carbohydrates turn slowly into energy, avoiding insulin production

A breakfast of muesli, nuts and yoghurt gives you a good ratio of protein and complex carbohydrate

A mid-morning snack tops up the intake of protein and complex carbohydrates

A combination of protein with simple and complex carbohydrates for lunch provides a steady flow of energy for the afternoon

You eat a typical breakfast of cereal and coffee – i.e. simple carbohydrates, sugar and caffeine

You have a "sensible" lunch, perhaps a pasta salad for energy or a green salad if you're *really* trying to shift some pounds, but there's no protein in your lunch

| KEY | Insulin production | Food Doctor dieter | Average dieter |
| --- | --- | --- | --- |

8am    9am    10am    11am    12pm    1pm

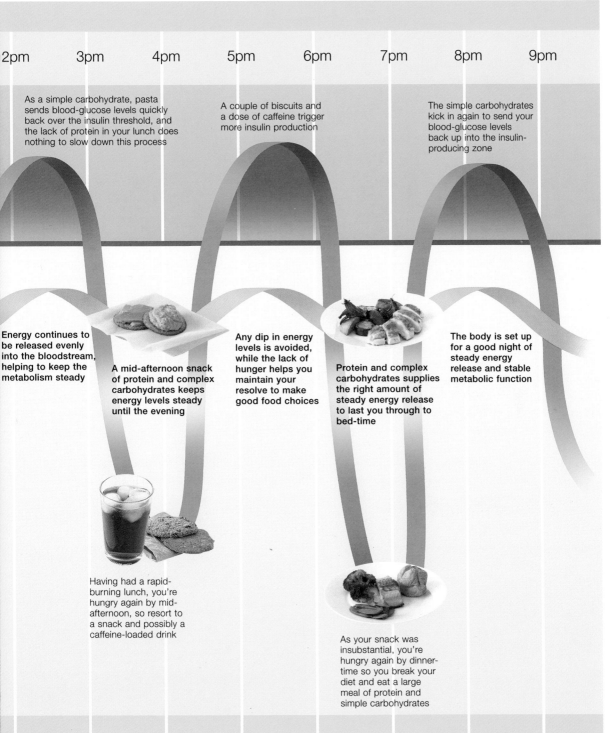

2pm  3pm  4pm  5pm  6pm  7pm  8pm  9pm

As a simple carbohydrate, pasta sends blood-glucose levels quickly back over the insulin threshold, and the lack of protein in your lunch does nothing to slow down this process

A couple of biscuits and a dose of caffeine trigger more insulin production

The simple carbohydrates kick in again to send your blood-glucose levels back up into the insulin-producing zone

Energy continues to be released evenly into the bloodstream, helping to keep the metabolism steady

A mid-afternoon snack of protein and complex carbohydrates keeps energy levels steady until the evening

Any dip in energy levels is avoided, while the lack of hunger helps you maintain your resolve to make good food choices

Protein and complex carbohydrates supplies the right amount of steady energy release to last you through to bed-time

The body is set up for a good night of steady energy release and stable metabolic function

Having had a rapid-burning lunch, you're hungry again by mid-afternoon, so resort to a snack and possibly a caffeine-loaded drink

As your snack was insubstantial, you're hungry again by dinner-time so you break your diet and eat a large meal of protein and simple carbohydrates

2pm  3pm  4pm  5pm  6pm  7pm  8pm  9pm

**Fibre** This slows the process of glucose extraction from other foods, which discourages rapid or excess glucose production and therefore reduces the need for the body to produce insulin.

To sum up, if you can eat in a way that focuses primarily on these "lows", glucose levels and insulin production will stay low, allowing fat to be released from the fats cells to make energy rather than encouraging fat to be stored. The 10 principles of The Food Doctor plan are designed to make it easy for you to achieve this.

The Food Doctor plan offers three ideal options for combining food groups that will minimise insulin production and thus minimise potential fat production too (see box, below right). There is a fourth, not-so-ideal option, which is to eat complex carbohydrates with fibre but without protein. This is the *least* preferable option because protein is the hardest food group to break down and therefore has the slowest glucose conversion rate, minimising the risk of triggering insulin production.

## Balancing your protein intake

A diet based largely on protein alone is a popular option, but not one I favour. I have put my plan together so that, when it is properly followed, it will always include the right sort of carbohydrates in each and every meal and snack. I believe that, although we are all different and the requirement for protein in each of us is different, when it comes to safe, consistent weight loss, we should all aim to eat a maximum of 40 per cent protein to minimise the risks associated with excess protein intake.

I find that people who follow high-protein diets tend not to eat the recommended five portions per day of fresh fruit and vegetables, which in turn means that their intake of antioxidants will probably be low. These vital substances are linked to reducing the risk of cancer, heart disease and arthritis. They also help to slow down the ageing process, so it's really not a good idea to exclude them from your food intake.

To be fair, most high-protein diets do encourage you to eat some fresh fruit and vegetables at a later stage in the diet, but my long experience with dieters tells me that a large proportion of them do not move on to that later stage. Instead, they stay in the all-fat and all-protein phase, as it requires little thought and there is less room for mistakes. It is at this induction phase that weight loss is most noticeable, but I maintain that this type of eating is not sustainable and, as such, it is just another diet with

a beginning, a middle and an end. So you "come off" the diet, or "cheat", and the weight reappears. The fact that many people eat this way highlights the sad fact that we choose to ignore what proper dieting can do. This tends to make us look at food only in terms of whether it can make us fat or thin.

Diets that rely on very high levels of protein can have several other potentially harmful effects:

**Fats** The type of protein eaten in high-protein diets is often very high in saturated fats – cheese, for example. Such fats, often called "bad" fats, block the absorption of the all-important essential fats. Eaten in excess, they may also raise cholesterol levels and thus increase the risk of cardiovascular disease.

**Calcium** Research suggests that there may be increased risks of kidney stones and osteoporosis if protein intake and calcium levels are excessive. Our bodies are designed to keep a balance between acid and alkaline, ensuring that the body's internal environment does not become too acid. Metabolising protein raises acidity and, if there is too much acid, it will be counteracted by the release of calcium from stores, in order to "buffer" the increased acidity. As most of the calcium in the body is held in the bones, a very high-protein diet can in the long term lead to decreased bone density. Calcium also has to be excreted and easily builds up in the kidneys. Here, it can form stones which, once broken down and passed through the urinary tract, can be excruciatingly painful.

**Fibre shortage** High-protein diets tend to be low in fibre, leading to constipation which in turn increases the risk of colon cancer.

**Sleep problems** There may be another, strange, side-effect of excess protein – on sleep. Proteins contain

---

### MAKING GOOD CHOICES

In The Food Doctor plan, there are three acceptable ways to combine the food groups:

1. Eat protein with vegetables and starchy complex carbohydrates.

2. Eat protein with vegetables.

3. Eat protein with just starchy complex carbohydrates (although this is the least preferable option with regard to the GI factor).

## A PERFECT COMBINATION

Protein and complex carbohydrates combine a good GI rating with a healthy intake of antioxidants and fibre.

40% protein
such as fish, lean meat or pulses

60% complex carbohydrates
such as green vegetables with plenty of fibre

amino acids, which are used everywhere in the body, including the most vital organ, the brain. Covering the brain is a porous layer of skin called the blood-brain barrier, which acts as a filter, allowing in some substances and protecting the brain from potential toxins. Because the barrier limits overall absorption, amino acids fight with one another for absorption. When carbohydrate is broken down in the body, amino acid levels are suppressed, with the exception of one, tryptophan, which is allowed through. This amino acid is effectively the precursor to sleep so, when excess protein is eaten without carbohydrates and other amino acid levels are not suppressed, tryptophan cannot pass unhindered into the brain to encourage sleep.

I have heard many people argue that surely all the risks and potential side-effects of excess protein is worth it for the promised weight loss, and surely obesity is just as much of a health risk as any of the other conditions. True, but there are ways of losing weight that do not involve such risks, and I feel that diets very high in protein and fat come with a potential price to pay that make them unnecessarily risky.

### The healthy way forward

Understanding the GI factor and learning how to fuel your body in a way that doesn't have negative side-effects, and doesn't distort your attitude to food, is what the Everyday Diet is about. High-protein or low-carbohydrate diets and low-calorie or low-fat diets all bring with them various problems (*see pp.42–43*). The 10 principles of The Food Doctor plan allow you to avoid the pitfalls associated with other common diets. Using these principles, you can establish a healthy eating

## Diets very **rich in protein** come with a potentially **high price** to pay for your **health**

pattern that controls insulin levels, avoids the insulin rollercoaster and eliminates the danger of disrupting your metabolism (*see pp.24–27*). In this way, it is a plan for life – one that is sustainable enough to last you a lifetime and practical enough to fit into your lifestyle.

# Key insulin triggers

By now you can see how important it is to keep blood-glucose levels as steady as possible. One of the main principles of The Food Doctor plan, "fuel up frequently", is designed to do just this. The amount you eat, how often you eat it, and the proportions of protein to complex carbohydrate in your meals all help to keep blood-glucose levels steady and avoid sending them over the insulin threshold. However, there are other key substances that can act as triggers to promote the release of insulin. Five of these key triggers – sugar, simple carbohydrates, stress, smoking and caffeine – are explained further here.

The term "insulin trigger" may sound quite alien to you, but these triggers are actually things that you may encounter daily without even thinking about it. Each of these insulin triggers have different characteristics in that some are sociable, some give you an energy boost, some are addictive – however they all involve the same sort of chemical change and reaction in your body when it comes to insulin production.

Insulin allows the body to store fat from the food you eat: without insulin this process is limited. Avoiding the insulin rollercoaster (*see pp.16–17*) is an important part of The Food Doctor plan, as this will help your body limit the amount of fat stored. Understanding the impact of the key triggers listed here, therefore, is vital to successfully controlling your weight.

### THE SCIENCE: ADRENALINE AND GLYCOGEN

Adrenaline is released to assist the body's reaction to a "flight or fight" situation. It is a throwback to our caveman days that can still be triggered by stress situations or stimulants. It has several effects, one of which is to divert blood from "secondary" areas such as the digestive system and pump it to areas primarily involved in flight or fight, such as the muscles, heart and lungs. Digestion is slowed, hindering absorption of nutrients and suppressing appetite. Blood-glucose levels climb rapidly to ensure that muscles have plenty of fuel to flee or fight. When the levels rise too high insulin is produced (*see pp.14–19*). The rapid rise is followed by a significant drop that triggers a demand for more energy – so you experience hunger.

## Sugar

Many years ago I read that as long as a food was fat-free then it would not contribute to excess weight. So I happily went out and bought lots of sweet, sugary foods that were effectively fat-free, and – guess what? – over a short period of time, I gained weight. I believe that fat was given a poor reputation years ago in terms of weight issues. Yet sugar, including honey, has been hiding quietly in the corner hoping that it wouldn't be noticed. It is time to bring the truth about sugar out into the open and recognise its negative role.

### What is sugar?
Sugar lurks in many forms: sucrose, mannitol, glucose, honey, lactose, fructose, sorbitol, corn syrup, malt, malt extract, maltose, rice syrup, rice extract, molasses, golden syrup and invert sugar are all pseudonyms for sugar. Refined sugar is a simple carbohydrate. In fact it is almost the epitome of one. As we know, simple carbohydrates are converted from food into glucose much more rapidly than their complex counterparts.

Sugar has only a few bonds to hold it together, making it free of fibre – the fibre that is important for slowing down glucose extraction.

Sugar, therefore, converts quickly into blood glucose, sending you rapidly over the insulin threshold (*see pp.16–17*).

Many of my clients proudly report that instead of eating "regular" chocolate they eat organic, healthy alternatives. I am pleased about this because it means they are reading food labels and hunting for good alternatives. Sadly, though, however you have it – organic, raw, brown or white – it is still sugar. It will still be converted into glucose with alarming speed and have the same effect on blood-glucose levels.

### What about honey?

After all, honey is natural, isn't it? Well, so is sugar – it grows in fields. Honey has acquired itself a romantic air: we think of bees buzzing around on a warm day collecting nectar and making honey in the hive for the genial bee-keeper to collect. It is true that honey has many beneficial health properties, but it is actually converted into glucose at almost the same speed as sugar. In fact, sugar (or saccharose) has a GI score of 70, whereas honey scores a massive 90.

### Better to go artificial?

Artificial sweeteners have a low GI score and therefore minimal effect on blood-glucose levels, but what concerns me is that "artificial" usually means "made from chemicals" and does not indicate any health benefits. Natural sweeteners, too, may have little effect on glucose levels, but they perpetuate the idea of eating sweet foods. If you can wean yourself off them, this is a much better option, and following the 10 principles should minimise any sugar cravings.

# Simple carbohydrates

Imagine eating a piece of mixed-grain bread – by this I mean one with visible whole grains. You have to chew it, mix it with your saliva and swallow it, allowing it to combine with the hydrochloric acid in your stomach. It passes into the digestive tract and the process of glucose extraction begins, along with the breakdown of vitamins and minerals. As this type of bread is a complex carbohydrate, it scores around 50 on the glycaemic index (*see pp.14, 47*).

Had you eaten white bread, which scores around 78 on the GI scale, the extraction of glucose would not have been slowed by the presence of whole grains. White-flour products have been over-processed until they lose their fibre – the fibre so essential for slowing down glucose extraction.

### What to avoid

You should minimise your intake of simple carbohydrates and avoid them when possible. So, reduce your intake of all sugars, many bread and flour products, cereals, white rice, white pasta, chocolate, confectionery, alcohol and sugary drinks. Alcohol is a simple carbohydrate and not only

causes the same changes to blood-glucose levels, but can also warp your concept of a good food choice. Try to limit your alcohol intake and have alcohol only with meals.

Another pitfall is breakfast cereals, as they break down rapidly. A typical dieter's low-calorie breakfast usually contains cereal, a glass of orange juice (after all, juice is healthy, isn't it?) and a cup of coffee (no milk as you are watching your weight). This gives you two simple carbohydrates and caffeine, all in your first meal of the day. No wonder you feel tired and hungry again by mid-morning.

### Juiced fruit and vegetables

On the subject of juices, one of the key values of fruit and vegetables lies in their fibre content. Health officials worldwide recommend that everyone eats at least five portions of fruit and vegetables every day, yet juice counts as just one portion. Even if you drink 10 glasses of juice a day, they still count as one portion. This is because, although a glass of juice contains vitamins and minerals, it has no fibre, yet fibre is just as important in combating disease as the antioxidants in fresh produce. In terms of The Food Doctor plan, the fibre is essential because it wraps around other foods and slows down the speed at which glucose is extracted. Whole foods, including fruits and vegetables, have far more intrinsic value than their derivatives.

Fruit juice, since it has no fibre to slow its conversion into glucose, has a high GI score, while whole fruit has a much lower score. If you like juicing, just ensure that you eat some of the whole fruit alongside your juice to slow down the speed at which it is turned into glucose.

# Stress

I can't imagine a life without stress. In fact, it is probably an impossibility. Even the most laid-back person is certain to experience some stress, however minimal. As I sit at my desk, working to meet deadlines, my stress levels are elevated, although I may be unaware of this. The chemical changes can be occuring in the body without you noticing them.

## The role of glycogen

The stress response is simple. When the body senses that stress or danger is present, it releases a hormone called adrenaline from the adrenal glands (*see box, p.20*). Adrenaline affects your blood-glucose levels, triggering the production of insulin that effectively encourages your body to lay down fat. Stress can therefore result in weight gain. Since adrenaline also inhibits digestion, it also prevents you from receiving all the nutrients you should from the foods you eat.

Stress has yet another way of affecting your weight. Adrenaline has the added effect of forcing stored glucose, known as glycogen, to be released from its stores in the muscles and liver. These glycogen stores are designed to provide quickly accessible short-term energy when needed during a stressful situation. The glycogen stores convert rapidly back into glucose and are released into the bloodstream to provide immediate energy to the muscles and brain which allows them to cope with the perceived stress or danger.

However, this glucose is not always needed, because common day-to-day stresses don't usually require us to flee or fight. This means that this surplus of glucose can then be stored, through a chain of biochemical changes, as fat.

## Recognising stress

Stress or danger can take many forms. It is not necessarily the sort of executive or work-place stress that so many of us associate with the word. In truth, anything you personally find stressful will trigger the stress response: from being late for the school run; behind on an important work project; worrying about a family situation, money issues or even weight problems. They all elicit the same response.

I am not suggesting that stress is something you can avoid, but do try to remember that it is one of the elements and influences that force glucose levels to rise, which in turn triggers insulin production. It may help explain why you may have gained weight recently.

If you are suffering from stress, I advise you to pay even more attention to how you are dealing with the other triggers, such as caffeine and refined sugar, because you may find that you will need to eliminate these completely to compensate for life's unavoidable stressful situations.

# Smoking

Cigarettes contain nicotine, a mild stimulant that triggers the release of adrenaline (*see box, p.20*), which impacts strongly on blood-glucose levels. I find that many smokers have problems managing their blood-glucose levels, but keeping them in check is, of course, an integral part of The Food Doctor plan.

## A poor start

Typically, a smoker may have their first cigarette at breakfast time, so blood-glucose levels spike right at the start of the day. I have also found that the majority of smokers skip breakfast because they have a cup of coffee and a cigarette instead. But breakfast sets the scene for the day. A small meal made from the right proportions of protein and complex carbohydrates effectively supplies fuel to encourage the metabolism to kick in for the day. Having a coffee and a cigarette instead will kill any feelings of needing food, so you eat less and your metabolism goes into "famine mode".

## Smoking and appetite

Most people are aware of the health risks associated with smoking, but I wonder how many people who smoke fully understand the link between smoking and excess weight. Traditionally smoking is seen as an appetite suppressant, and surely that makes it a good thing for dieters? It is not that simple, I'm afraid. Aside from the link with rising and falling levels in blood-glucose, there is the problem that smoking reduces and sometimes completely removes the desire to eat. Then, when you quit smoking (which hopefully one day you will), your appetite returns and you find yourself eating much more than your metabolism is used to (*see pp.24–27*). The good news is that keeping glucose levels in check through regular eating, as advocated in The Food Doctor plan, can significantly reduce the level at which ex-smokers need to replace nicotine with food when they give up.

At the risk of preaching, I ask my clients who come in for private consultations if they intend to smoke for the rest of their lives. Invariably, their answer is no. So then I ask when they expect the rest of their lives to begin. This is trite, I know, but it does help them focus their minds on why they continue to smoke.

### How this diet helps
If you are a committed smoker, I suggest you keep a record by writing down the times of day you normally have a cigarette. Then try eating little and often during the day, especially at those particular times when you usually have a cigarette break, still bearing in mind my recommended ratios of complex carbohydrates and protein. You may well find that your dependence on nicotine diminishes naturally and this makes quitting the habit altogether a far easier task than you might have imagined.

# Caffeine

Caffeine is found most commonly in drinks such as coffee and cola. To a slightly lesser degree it is also present in tea and chocolate. Energy drinks are, of course, further significant sources.

These days, coffee-drinking seems to have become an integral feature of daily life: we're often grabbing a cappuccino or latte en route to work, or meeting a friend for a mid-morning coffee at one of the many coffee shops that have sprung up in our towns.

Coffee (and therefore caffeine) has become a social phenomenon, and drinking coffee repeatedly during the day has become the norm. But how does this seemingly innocuous beverage affect our weight?

### Highs and lows
Caffeine stimulates the production of adrenaline (*see box, p.20*) and can be addictive because of the "highs" and "lows" that follow. When adrenaline levels are elevated, we feel awake and able to work and function well. However, this feeling is always followed by a slump once the effect of the adrenaline wears off. This leaves us feeling sluggish and weary because we are no

longer able to sustain that high. The rise in blood-glucose levels, inevitably followed by a fall, leaves the coffee-drinker in that familiar position of feeling hungry or in need of more caffeine to try to recreate the high. Either way, no-one, no matter how focused and strong-willed he or she may be, is likely to make great food choices in this situation because they feel tired and in need of a boost. Can you imagine craving some green vegetables and houmous mid-morning after a breakfast of cereal and coffee? It is fairly improbable, isn't it? You are far more likely to crave a biscuit or three, plus another cup of coffee.

### Coffee and weight control
Coffee is readily available and popping out for a latte has become more than socially acceptable, it is positively sociable.

I rarely drink coffee as I am aware of its negative effects, but I recognise that its social associations have rendered excessive coffee-drinking apparently innocuous. Coffee is still a stimulant, however, and you must start thinking of it in that way. If you want to lose weight easily, consistently and long-term, then reducing your intake of caffeine has to be part of the whole life-changing process. If you really feel you can't cut it out completely, limit yourself to only one cup of coffee a day.

Keeping glucose levels in check by eating little and often, and eating protein together with complex carbohydrates at every meal, including snacks, will minimise cravings and curb any desire for stimulants – including caffeine.

# Your metabolism

People often blame their metabolisms for their failure to lose weight, and it's true that the metabolism is a key factor in successful weight control. Understanding the impact of repeated dieting on your metabolism will help you avoid the pitfalls in future.

I deal with clients who have a wide range of issues, but when it comes to those who seek advice solely for weight loss I will always ask them which diets they have tried. The usual response is "all of them". Of course they will have lost weight on all the diets they did but, needless to say, once they stop the restrictive way of eating prescribed by whichever diet they're trying and return to their normal eating habits, they gain back all the weight they lost and more. Sound familiar? This sort of dieting history can usually be traced back to being a teenager or young adult, and the most difficult part is helping clients understand that The Food Doctor plan is not actually a diet. I tell them that is the end of their "dieting" days, and I draw diagrams such as the insulin rollercoaster (*see pp.16–17*) and the six steps to a confused metabolism flowchart (*see overleaf*), and explain why the approaches they have tried so far have been unsuccessful in keeping their weight down in the long term.

When I first started incorporating this information into weight-loss consultations I found that people reacted quite strongly. The most usual response was one of familiarity and sometimes frustration at having been "on" diets for so long. There have been tears, nods of understanding or smiles as the story seems too close to home. Let me explain why that is, and how repeated dieting might have led you to this point in your life.

## Your metabolic "set point"

We all have a "set point". This is the point at which your food intake creates exactly the same amount of glucose (*see p.26*) as your body requires for its day-to-day functioning. For example, let's assume that your set point is 2000 calories: the daily energy your body needs to walk, talk, digest, breathe and think is 2000 calories, which is equal to the amount your body produces from the food you consume in an average

day. I don't usually like to think or refer to food in terms of its calorific value but it is useful in this context for ease of reference.

## How dieting affects your set point

Now, what happens to your set point when you alter that balance? As outlined below and illustrated overleaf, dieting doesn't have the impact you'd like on your metabolism.

If we assume, for instance, that over time you have exceeded your energy requirements and have stored some fat, so you decide to go "on a diet" and cut down your calorie intake. You know that exercise burns calories, so you join a gym, take up running, start walking to work, or get off the bus a couple of stops earlier than you need to, to burn off more calories than you're eating.

So now your body has to release some of its stored glucose to meet the new exercise demand and compensate for your decision to decrease your calories. Once the glycogen runs out, fat stores are mobilised to turn the food that was stored away back into energy. So you lose a bit of weight in the first week or so although, as any long-term dieter will probably know, glycogen is stored in water so the weight you lose early on is the water that the glycogen was held in. But there's a bigger problem brewing. Your metabolism doesn't realise you are living in the 21st century. It thinks you are a caveman or cavewoman. So it assumes that you are hitting a period of famine and compensates by going into "famine mode" (*see overleaf*), slowing itself down a little and lowering its set point to meet the new level of food intake.

Now you will find that your weight loss slows or even stops, which is pretty frustrating because a few days beforehand you'd been convinced that the diet

## THE BENEFITS OF EXERCISE

- Enhances metabolic rate and helps you burn body fat.

- Increases blood flow and helps improve cardiovascular function.

- Helps overall glucose management and tolerance, which reduces the need for insulin.

- Reduces blood pressure.

- Encourages endorphin creation, which relieves anxiety and improves mood.

was working and worth sticking to. It is at this point that you are tempted to "break" the diet or "cheat", as you feel a little let down. Let's assume, however, that you are being strong-willed, and you decide to cut down a little more, and increase the exercise too. Your weight loss speeds up again, but sadly, the set point lowers further as your food intake has dropped yet again. So now that your set point has lowered, your body has adjusted to a very restricted level of food intake and you need to stick that just to stay at exactly the same weight. This is not sustainable, enjoyable or flexible and,

worse still, is unlikely to provide you with much energy. At this point you will start to get hungry, and so begins the cycle of self-blame and guilt for being hungry, or for being unable to control yourself (see p.30). For long-term dieters this tale is sadly familiar, but the lesson applies to everyone, long-term dieters and new ones alike – lose weight slowly at a sustainable rate if you want to be successful and avoid disrupting your metabolism.

### But what about the Seven-day Diet?

So, if dieting messes up the set point, why did I devise the Seven-day Diet in my previous book, *The Food Doctor Diet*? What is so different about it? Well, I included it as a "starter diet" for several reasons. The primary reason was to promote digestive health, and to introduce you to the 10 principles (see pp.12–13) in a structured way that showed you how easy it can be to follow them.

The Seven-day Diet is lower in calories than my Plan for Life (in the previous book) and the Everyday Diet here. While it is a structured diet, you can be flexible about it if you prefer. There is no magic to it, just plain good sense and an ideal balance so, should you prefer to eat the food for day 6 on day 3, or swap lunch for dinner on a specific day, or generally change meals around to suit your preferences, it doesn't matter: the most important elements stay the same.

So why is it different from other diets and why won't it mess up your set point? Simply because it still follows the 10 principles, it still guarantees sustained energy release throughout the day, and it's designed to last for a limited period only. The Seven-day Diet is not just about reducing calories, it's about eating the right foods little and often. You're never starving or short of fuel, so your body never retreats into famine mode. Ideally you should be aiming to follow the 10 principles in the long term, with the Seven-day Diet as a "kick-start" or "booster" option. I recommend that you do not follow the Seven-day Diet for longer than a week at a time, and do not repeat the Seven-day Diet more than once every six weeks. By doing this you will avoid upsetting your set point and not risk encouraging your metabolism to store away an increased level of your food as fat.

### How exercise affects your set point

Often, just as people set themselves unachievable goals with diets that are unsustainable, they also try to maintain exercise routines that are equally unrealistic.

Gyms actually rely on the vast majority of their members *not* to come and, aside from every January, they usually get it right. Taking out a gym membership at the start of the year is just like starting a new diet, and often the two happen together. But by February, when your resolve has weakened as real life gets in the way, your food intake will revert to a previous pattern, and you won't be able to keep up the gym visits either. So another situation occurs in which you're setting yourself up to feel as though you've "failed" (*see p.30*).

It is absolutely true that we should exercise to enhance weight loss, but it helps to understand what happens in terms of metabolism when it comes to exercising. If we remind ourselves that food becomes glucose, which circulates in the blood and enters cells to be used as fuel to create energy, then we can see that the more energy we require, the more glucose we will utilise. So surely the more we exercise, or the harder we do it, the more fat we will burn? No, not quite. All too often clients come to me specifically to lose weight and complaining that, aside from eating very little, they have also been exercising frantically each day. I hear tales of hour-long cardiovascular workouts, or 45 minutes sweating it out on treadmills or in aerobic classes, yet without the weight loss that you might expect from such exertion. And how many of you have been confused at the gym to find that one of the *lower* rather than higher settings on the machines is the one for "fat-burning"? I could never understand why it took a lower output of energy to burn fat – surely the faster you exercised, the more weight you would lose?

## SIX STEPS TO A CONFUSED METABOLISM

We all have a "set point" – a point at which your food intake creates exactly the same glucose as your body requires for its day-to-day functioning. In terms of weight control, it means that you don't lose or gain a single pound or gram that day.

**Your first diet**
So, for example, you have a metabolic set point of 2000 calories, but you're feeling a little plump so you decide to lose a bit of weight ...

**Cut calories**
To do this, you go on a quick crash-diet, lowering your intake to 1750 calories and increasing your exercise levels to 2250 calories ...

**Quick fix**
In a fair world, you'd lose weight due to the 500-calorie difference in food intake and energy burned – and for a week or two you do, as your set point hasn't yet adjusted to the reduced calorie intake and stays at 2000. But life isn't that fair ...

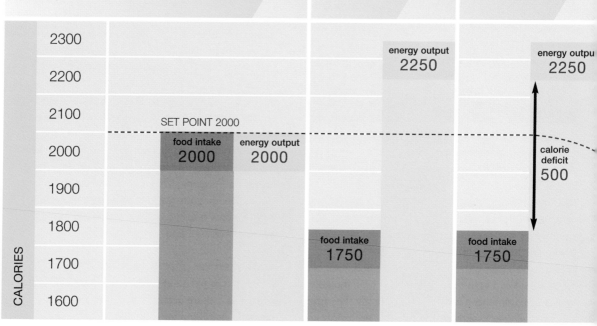

Unfortunately, it seems that, just as your set point can adapt to reduced food intake, so it may equally well be able to adapt to expect high levels of exercise. Your metabolism adjusts so that your body can sustain these levels without burning any extra calories. Therefore just as under-eating can have an effect on your set point, so can over-exercising.

## How to achieve a stable set point

Rather than frenetic over-exercising, it is actually sustained medium-level output (the "slow burn") that is important for enhancing your set point and encouraging the gentle and sustained release of fat, allowing it to be turned back into glucose so that your body can use it for energy.

The best way to do an exercise programme is to find an achievable balance, an exercise you enjoy and a regime you can follow even when you are short of time. This may mean joining a gym, or getting together with a few friends to exercise, or just walking for a certain amount of time each day. The vital factor is to find something that you can slot into your life with ease and enjoyment. Don't allow exercise to become a huge hurdle to losing weight.

There is only one way to lose weight sensibly and slowly. That is to eat little and often, combining complex carbohydrates and protein as recommended in The Food Doctor plan – and to exercise at a steady level. This will ensure that your set point is maintained and avoid triggering your body's famine response.

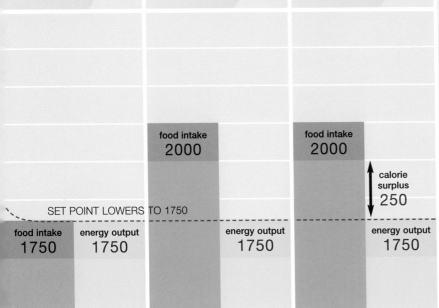

**Set point adjusts**
After a few days, your restricted food intake of only 1750 calories triggers a "potential famine" alert in your body, which adjusts to function on that level by lowering its set point. You are eating only 1750 calories a day, but your body has adjusted to fulfill all your energy demands on only that amount of calories ...

**After the diet**
You struggle to maintain a limited food intake of only 1750 calories a day, so you finish your diet and go back up to your "normal" intake of 2000 calories ...

**Famine mode**
BUT, as your set point is now only 1750, your body has a surplus of 250 calories. This is compounded by the fact that, as your body is in famine mode, it efficiently maximises this excess into a glucose surplus. As energy output is only 1750, this surplus is stored as FAT ...

**The end result ...**
When you were dieting, your metabolism was alerted to possible famine and reset itself. Off the diet and in a time of relative abundance, it will store more of the food you eat as fat rather than make energy with it, in preparation for the next famine. The end result is that you gain back the weight you lost, and more.

To repair the damage long-term dieting causes your set point and adjust it back upwards, you need a regular, steady supply of fuel combined with medium-level, sustained exercise. How quickly your set point recovers depends on many factors, such as the length and frequency of your diets, together with your caffeine intake and stress levels.

food intake
2000

food intake
2000

calorie surplus
250

SET POINT LOWERS TO 1750

food intake
1750

energy output
1750

energy output
1750

energy output
1750

# Think differently
## Portion proportion

For long-term dieters, or even for those who may be starting their very first diet, one issue that comes up frequently is that of just how much food they should be eating. Many people are worried about over-eating, and I can understand their concern.

I find that all too often long-term dieters cannot trust themselves not to over-eat, which is why they can be so attracted to diets that cut out almost entire food groups. With such diets they feel that, even if they do over-eat, they are still "safe" as long as they stick to the permitted food groups.

Over-eating and guilt and failure go hand-in-hand. Traditional diets that restrict your food intake reinforce the whole scenario of "right" and "wrong", "good" and "bad" – a scenario that makes them unsustainable and inevitably doomed to failure (*see pp.30–31*).

### The ideal combination
When you understand the 10 simple principles of The Food Doctor plan (*see pp.12–13*) and, most importantly, eat frequently and combine the food groups in the ideal ratios, there is little danger of over-eating. The combination of ratios and timing will

## HOW IT ALL ADDS UP

| | BREAKFAST | MID-MORNING |
|---|---|---|
| **AVERAGE DIETER**<br><br>Many people follow what seems to be a healthy diet and, on the face of it, their food intake looks fine. There's nothing wrong with the foods, it's just the timing and the ratios that are wrong, resulting in blood-glucose lows, insulin production and hunger. | 25%<br><br><br><br>muesli with dried fruit, nuts and chopped pear | +0%<br><br>mid-morning hunger |
| **FOOD DOCTOR DIETER**<br><br>Fuelling up frequently doesn't involve eating more than the average dieter, just spreading out the same food intake and eating the right foods at the right time to maintain the body's energy supply and avoid the insulin rollercoaster (*see pp.16–17*). | 20%<br><br><br><br>muesli with dried fruit and nuts (fewer nuts than above) | +10%<br><br><br><br>chopped pear with the remaining nuts from breakfast |

automatically ensure that your meals and snacks will be large enough to satisfy you and supply the correct amount of glucose to see you through to the next meal (*see pp.18–19*). By adopting the 10 principles, you can avoid over-eating as you are not compensating for having been "bad" by skipping breakfast, for instance, or making up for the fact that you know you are planning to over-eat that evening.

## Eat frequently

For many dieters the idea of eating five times a day might seem a little alarming, as they are so used to limiting their food intake and feeling hungry. However, following The Food Doctor plan doesn't necessarily involve eating more food, it just

means spreading it out more evenly through the day (*see chart, below*). This ensures that blood-glucose levels stay even, energy is steadily released, and the body isn't pushed over the insulin threshold (*see pp.18–19*).

## Use your hands

You're probably familiar with those tedious diets that tell you exactly how many segments of grapefruit or slices of cucumber you can eat, regardless of your size, build or gender. The Food Doctor plan makes it so much easier: instead of counting out each bit of food, you use your hands as a guide to your portion size (*see box, right*). For each meal, I give the portion sizes of each food group as a percentage of your hands' surface area (*see for example p.46*).

### A HANDS-ON APPROACH

Using hands as a portion guide works for us all, large or small, since hands are generally in proportion to bodies. For each meal I suggest simple portion sizes based on hand size.

| LUNCH | MID-AFTERNOON | DINNER |
|---|---|---|
| +35% | +0% | +40%   =100% |

mid-afternoon hunger

salad of red pepper, goat's cheese, avocado, leaves and pine nuts

salmon with pea mash, steamed vegetables and new potatoes

| +30% | +10% | +30%   =100% |

as above, but with potatoes: save some goat's cheese and red pepper

rice cracker with the reserved goat's cheese and red pepper

as above, but without the new potatoes, which you had for lunch

# Are you a "good" dieter?

Today, far too many of us think – consciously or subconsciously – that being slim is the sign of a good person. Conversely, being overweight is a sign that we are bad, or greedy, or out of control. We apply this judgement to such an extent that the word "fat" is an insult.

We can use the word fat to sabotage ourselves, implying that, being fat, we are also bad or greedy.

### The power of words
This attitude leads to the kind of dieting that invites the use of words and phrases like "good" and "bad", "cheat", "fall off the wagon", "start again on Monday" – I am sure you know them all. I cannot emphasise enough the value of taking a long, hard look at the words and phrases you use to describe yourself, and the way you talk about your dieting. You may well find that you are reinforcing a negative view of yourself and a distorted view of food and what it does for you.

Think how easy it is to make yourself feel bad when it comes to dieting and food choices. For example, you say things to yourself like "I should eat an apple mid-morning – after all, I am on a diet, but I want something else really." But, as you are on a diet, you deny yourself. A few minutes later you might think "I'll have raisins, after all, that's fruit so it's healthy." A few minutes later still you might think "I'll get the yoghurt-covered raisins

– after all, yoghurt is good for you, isn't it?" But in truth your choice is sugar masquerading as a snack. So you "ruin" your diet and, after a process of denial and indulgence, the "guilt" sets in and you think that you have ruined the whole diet for today anyway, so you may as well just eat "normally" and start "dieting" again tomorrow.

If you follow The Food Doctor plan, and eat at the right times in the ideal proportion, however, then you can get off the diet treadmill – and leave behind the language that goes with it – once and for all.

### Another layer of guilt
Exercise is another area in which we can set ourselves up to fail. Often, when people start a new diet, they galvanise themselves into action at the gym too. So alongside unrealistic and unsustainable diets, people try to maintain exercise routines that are equally unrealistic. But soon the real world gets in the way and the demands of work and family makes inroads into your exercise time, just as it does on the time you set aside for food preparation. When this happens, you revert back to your old

eating patterns and forego the gym visits. So another situation arises in which you're setting yourself up to feel as though you've "failed".

### The 80:20 rule
One of my 10 principles that people never have trouble remembering is the 80:20 rule – the principle that, as long as you follow The Food Doctor plan for 80 per cent of the time, you can "stray" for 20 per cent of the time. This principle allows for the Real World, and it acknowledges that there may be times when you *really* want chocolate, for instance. That doesn't mean you're a "failure" or that you've "ruined" your diet: it's done, so just pick up and carry on with The Food Doctor plan at your next meal. As the plan isn't a "diet", you don't "fall off" it: it's an eating plan for life, and it's always there in the background to help you make good food choices.

### On the right lines
Many of us try hard to be "good" and to stay on track. We've picked up various words of wisdom during the course of our dieting years and we feel "good" if we follow them. Sadly, many of these are myths (*see opposite*) and will only sabotage your attempts at weight loss – setting yourself up for more frustration and possibly even comfort-eating if your dieting cycle is particularly vicious.

Unless you feel the same **longing for broccoli**, the magnesium-craving theory isn't a viable **excuse for chocolate**

## "I eat lots of fruit"

Fresh fruit is an excellent source of fibre, liquid, minerals and vitamins, including essential antioxidants. However, do bear in mind that it is also rich in fructose, which is a type of sugar, albeit one with a relatively low GI value. Keep fruit intake under control, especially soft fruits, and ensure that there is no shortfall in nutrient intake by making sure you eat plenty of fresh vegetables.

## "I never eat eggs"

The high cholesterol content of eggs scares many people, but eggs are a complete protein food and, when poached, scrambled or lightly boiled, they make an excellent companion for complex carbohydrates. The fat in eggs is low in saturates so it counts as "good" fat. All in all, eggs fit well within The Food Doctor plan and are especially versatile.

## "I only have cravings for chocolate when I have PMS"

There is a theory that women crave foods rich in magnesium, e.g. chocolate, to help ease PMS. However, green vegetables also contain magnesium so, unless you feel equally desperate for broccoli, the magnesium-craving theory does not seem to hold. Sugar cravings can be minimised by following the 10 principles.

## "I only have salad for lunch"

Not all salads are created equal, and a traditional dieter's lunch-time salad, usually some lettuce, tomatoes and cucumber, simply doesn't provide enough food intake. It is a very low-calorie meal that lacks any protein. As we know, however, you need higher levels of fuel to maintain your metabolic rate and avoid lowering your set point (see pp.24–27).

## "I love fruit juice"

Many dieters think that fruit juice will help them lose weight. If you squeeze your own juice, you will be familiar with the fibrous mess that you throw away. That fibre is as important as the juice and losing it is not part of my plan. If you do drink juice, always have it *in addition to* your regular fibre intake (that is, vegetables and whole grains). Don't replace main meals with smoothies or juices – this will not help weight loss at all.

## "I've inherited a sweet tooth from my parents"

Some people do, of course, prefer sweet to savoury foods, but inheriting a sweet tooth is unlikely. It is more likely that your sweet tooth is due to habit and upbringing rather than genes. Following the 10 principles keeps blood-glucose levels even, which makes you less likely to want to indulge your sweet tooth.

## "I only drink black, sugar-free coffee"

Holding back on the sugar may seem virtuous, but there's another problem with coffee – its caffeine content. Caffeine is the dieter's enemy: it encourages glucose levels to rise, which affects your metabolic rate as well as triggering insulin production. This, as we know, will in turn encourage fat storage (see p.23).

## "I always choose red wine"

Most red wines are relatively rich in the nutrients that benefit the heart, so they're a "good" choice for dieters. However, alcohol has a high GI score and converts into glucose quite rapidly, so drink wine only with your meals, not before them. One or two glasses three times a week is enjoyable and acceptable on The Food Doctor plan (see p.145).

## "Spreads are healthier than butter"

In most diets butter is a villain and spreads are king. But some spreads are better than others – how do you know which are "good"? While many are fine, some are very artificial. I prefer the real thing – regular butter every time, in moderation of course, and preferably unsalted. It is tasty, and will not overly upset The Food Doctor plan.

# Don't count calories

Are you one of those people who judges all food – without even realising you do it – by its calorific value? If you regard food as calories and make your decisions about what to eat based solely on calorie content, then your food choices may not be healthy ones.

The calorie-counting method of eating fails to take into account the true value of food. While I am not unaware of the calorie content of food, I do feel that the value of food lies in more than just the number of calories it contains. In my clinic I have worked with a number of clients who can recount the calorie content of any food from memory. All their choices about what to eat are based around this, but in my opinion that gives rise to two serious issues: their relationship with food and their criteria for judging its value (*see also pp.42–43*).

### An unhealthy relationship
Firstly, food can end up becoming an obsession. What should I eat today? Have I had too many calories? Should I be saving some for later? If this is you, then ask yourself: how well has this approach actually served you up to now? Are you the weight you want to be, or do you still battle? Do you slide off the wagon sometimes and indulge in ice-cream or pizza, and then feel guilty for not being able to control yourself? If so, where does that leave you? In my experience, it makes you feel as if

you have failed, and nothing is more likely to send you back to making poor food choices than feeling bad about yourself (*see pp.30–31*).

Then there is the problem of the reduced-calorie foods available. Take a look at the list of ingredients in a typical ready-made low-calorie meal and you will see elements that you wouldn't add if you were making the same meal at home, such as modified starch, salt and preservatives. Low-calorie meals tend to be processed and sugared – the opposite of what I feel smart eating is all about.

### The true value of food
Calories are one way of measuring what you are eating, but if you make your food choices based solely on whether a food will make you fatter or thinner, then – to be blunt – you have lost the plot. The foods that will enhance your health and digestion and keep the body functioning at optimum levels are not necessarily those that are low in calories. This doesn't mean you should ignore their calorie values, but rather make it just one of the ways in which you choose what to eat instead of it being the first and most important factor.

Here's an example. If you're focusing purely on calories, you might choose low-calorie cereal with skimmed milk, black coffee and juice for breakfast. However, these are all notoriously low in fibre and protein and rich in simple carbohydrates, which leads to them being converted from food into glucose rapidly. Since this provides only short-term energy, it is highly likely that you'll be hungry again by mid-morning. The rest of the morning is then spent trying not to eat, or berating yourself for being hungry ("What's wrong with me?" "Why can't I control myself, it's only a couple of hours until lunch?"). If you had ignored the calorie count and instead eaten a breakfast that included fibre and protein, such as muesli with nuts and seeds, or even peanut butter on toast, the foods would have broken down into glucose more slowly and provided energy for longer to avoid both the hunger and also the common mid-morning dilemma – whether or not you can eat again soon.

My advice is: put calories to the back of your mind and choose your food based on a way of eating that will serve you better in the long run. In time, it will become second nature (just as counting calories did). Foods can then be judged in terms of taste, consistency and – most importantly – nutritional value. Let food work for you, not the other way around.

**Healthy food** is not necessarily **low-calorie food**, yet that is how many of us define the **value** of **what we eat**

# Calories versus nutrients

If you've been counting calories for some time, you probably haven't eaten an avocado in ages, since it is high in calories. But that ignores its nutritional value. A low-calorie dieter might favour the diet drink with zero calories, but with zero nutrition too (*see below*).

Dieters who count calories can fall into the trap of viewing food merely as the sum of its calorific value, with nutritional value ignored. This leads to poor food choices. For example, oily fish that is full of essential fats and vitamins would be ignored in favour of "spending" the calories on food with fewer calories in it.

### Diet drink
The diet drink may have no calories, but it is also "empty" of any value in terms of nutritional benefits. It is also likely to be packed with chemicals and caffeine.

energy 0.4kcal
protein 0g
fibre 0g

### Avocado
The calories in an avocado come from its mono-unsaturated fats, which are important for healthy body function. An avocado also contains other nutrients such as potassium and vitamins A, E and B[6], making it full of "nutritional" calories.

energy 340kcal
protein 4.8g
fibre 16.2g

# Everyday eating

Here you will find all the essential tools you need to be able to make smart food choices in every given situation: at work; at home; in a hurry; out with friends; at breakfast, lunch, dinner, or when snacking. With more than 100 recipes to choose from and many more ideas and variations to browse through, this part of the book shows you how easy it is to follow The Everyday Diet.

# Buying good food

There are so many confusing labels out there and so much clever packaging designed to make you feel good about what you're buying. But will it actually help you to control your weight and maintain it? Here's my guide to the shopping maze.

There's no doubt about it: preparing your own food from scratch is the safest way to ensure that there are no "hidden extras" in your meals. But, in the real world, we are often short of time and desperate for convenient options, particularly if they offer a promise of weight loss too. That's when we fall prey to the pitfalls of shopping and make poor choices in our food selections.

### Always read the label

When you first start with The Food Doctor plan try to take a little extra time to shop, looking at the foods you usually buy. Check the labels for their carbohydrate, fat and sugar listings. Watch out for modified starch and high salt content. Avoid the many forms of sugar that are innocently hidden behind names such as sorbitol, malt extract or corn syrup. There are more than 16 ways to

## Lack of **time** to shop or cook **doesn't have** to mean lack of **good food**

describe sugar (*see p.20*), and it's the same story for fats. The trick is to look for the healthy, essential fats derived from sources such as seeds, nuts, plants and oily fish, and to avoid the saturated and trans fats (often listed as hydrogenated or partially hydrogenated vegetable oils).

The food industry aims to make its products appealing, so claims such as "reduced fat", "low-fat" and "lite" are littered around to tempt you to buy anything from ready-made meals to a simple carton of yoghurt. In reality, many of these claims are not regulated by law. Nor do these products necessarily contain fewer calories or "healthier" ingredients: in many cases, where the fat comes out, sugar goes in to give the product taste and substance.

Since one of my 10 principles (*see pp.12–13*) is to avoid sugar, foods labelled as "no added sugar" might seem tempting. Again, however, beware, as this simply means that sugar has not been added as an extra ingredient: it does not mean there is no sugar present in the product.

### The food industry

So how have things come to this? Why all the tricks and misleading labelling? The blame lies equally with the food industry and with ourselves. I know that food manufacturers come in for a lot of criticism, and I feel that it's generally with good reason. Like any business, however, they have a right to make a profit and to run their business in a manner that reduces their costs and maximises their profit. They are often public companies and therefore have an obligation to their shareholders to be successful. The food manufacturers make foods that are saleable, and so they make them as rich in flavour as they can (which can mean added salt, sugar or other additives), and use ingredients that are consistently available and have "added value". This means that, for example, while a simple potato is worth a few pennies, if you chop it finely, deep fry it in oil, add some salt and package it in shiny brightly coloured foil, that same potato is a crisp worth many times more than the original. Throw in some celebrity advertising and suddenly the potato is a potential pot of gold.

The same can be said for the ears of corn that become a breakfast cereal, nuts that get honey-coated and roasted, simple meal recipes that become high-value ready-made meals (with instructions to "pierce film several times and ensure product is hot before serving") or fruit that is juiced, mixed with yoghurt and turned into a smoothie. Due to the high profit margin, the food manufacturers can afford heavy advertising, often with celebrity endorsement, that suggests that their product and their product alone will help you lose weight, or is a great alternative to a cooked breakfast for those of us who are short on time, or whatever.

In this way, the food industry has to a large extent influenced what we all weigh. OK, so they may have taken a few liberties with exact truths over the years, allowing us to think that the phrase "low-fat" on a packet would result in us being low in fat, or suggesting that a carbonated, caffeinated, artificially sweetened drink deserved the word "diet" in its title, but all they really gave us was what we wanted. And what we wanted was food that was going to keep us healthy, full, satisfied and thin, yet could be prepared in seconds with little effort or thought on our part. No easy task.

Our own role in the food industry cannot be under-estimated. We have contradictory attitudes. As well as expecting food to be cheap and available all year round, we want it to be good for us. Yet we will pay more for fatty, sugared and salted added-value foods, because we are too busy to cook. Food scares outrage us, yet our high expectations of the food industry makes it almost inevitable that quality may suffer from time to time.

## A question of time

The time factor is of great relevance when it comes to weight loss. I realise we are all busy, and that life today brings endless pressures, but when people consult me for weight loss, it often turns out that they have been using convenience foods as staple foods. Low-fat snacks and ready-made meals allow them time for other things and, with so much else to do in life aside from worry about food, it's easy to see how tempting it can be to believe the labels and try the short-cuts. But resorting to such processed foods is not going to provide the answers: only sensible eating can do that.

I firmly believe that, if we can learn the principles of good eating, then we can start to enjoy food properly. By putting food higher up the list of priorities than it is, and by apportioning time to cook and prepare food, we can make better choices affecting our weight and overall health. It doesn't have to be disruptive to your life (many of the recipes in this book can be made in only 10 minutes or so). It simply means ensuring that you have a healthy attitude to food, you are organised in your shopping, and you keep the 10 principles in mind when you prepare meals. Lack of time doesn't have to mean lack of good food (*see also pp.36–37*).

## HELP YOURSELF

Willpower and motivation are all very well, but simply the act of food shopping can cause the most determined of us to waver. Make shopping easier on yourself with the following tips:

- We've all heard the one about not shopping when you're hungry, but it's a good rule. If you can avoid shopping when you're already hungry you'll find it much easier to make good food choices.

- If you know the layout of your supermarket, you know which aisles are full of biscuits and crisps. Just don't let yourself go down those aisles – mysteriously no biscuits will end up in your shopping basket.

- Try to make a list of what you need before you go shopping and stick to the items on it (*see pp.44–45 for the "perfect" shopping list*), but don't be blind to interesting new foods. You could aim to add one new food a week to your shopping basket – just be sure to make healthy choices.

- If time allows, don't let food shopping become a dull, routine chore. Shopping at farm shops, greengrocers, butchers, etc, will help you avoid the lure of the racks crammed with sugary, fatty foods and ready-made meals.

# Compare and contrast

There are so many different diets to try, but how well do they work and what are the health costs? In our eagerness to find a simple weight solution many of us embrace diets that are, in fact, unhealthy.

There is a wide range of diets on the market, many of which can be very hard to follow and impossible to stick to. Many focus on calorie-counting or excluding certain food groups. So if someone tells you of a different diet that allows you those forbidden foods, then of course it's tempting – all those foods that have been off your list could be on it again. The problem is that you are still on a diet, with its own list of forbidden foods. So, inevitably, after a while, you will start to crave the foods that your new diet does not allow.

Ultimately I feel that any "diet" is doomed to fail, since by its nature it has a beginning, middle and end, and is something you try as an *alternative* to your usual eating patterns rather than as an *improvement* on them. The Food Doctor plan, in contrast, includes all food groups. I'd like you to avoid sugar, but even that isn't forbidden, thanks to the 80:20 rule (*see pp.12–13*). The balance between the food groups means that no foods are off-limits, so cravings will be minimal.

The problem with low-calorie and high-protein diets is that they distort your concept of the value of food, which becomes merely the sum of its calorific value or carbohydrate content. Thus, for instance, the essential fats that your body needs for optimum health and for weight loss are labelled as "fattening" and avoided by low-calorie dieters, who prefer to "spend" their calories on eating more food with a lower value. Faced with a choice between a few nuts or a few low-calorie biscuits, they choose the latter and forget that the nuts supply essential fats promoting weight loss and healthy hair, skin and nails, while the biscuits are full of sugar, which may be "low-fat" but which have a very high GI score (*see p.14*). A comparison of two other diets with The Food Doctor plan shows clearly its benefits (*see right*).

## The Food Doctor plan

### PROMISE

An eating plan for life, with no deprivation, hunger pangs or calorie-counting. No food group is excluded, and there is a healthy balance of fibre, protein and complex carbohydrates to ensure optimum health.

### OUTCOME

- As no food group is excluded, the plan provides balanced nutrition for optimum health.

- Eating regular meals promotes a stable metabolism and avoids hunger, with its inherent dangers to willpower and food choices.

- Intake of fruit and vegetables is high, ensuring plenty of fibre and antioxidant consumption.

- Its practical, realistic eating pattern means that you're unlikely to "cheat" or find it too hard to do, and it's a plan for life, so you don't have to stop.

- You are encouraged to eat "healthy" fats such as the essential fats derived from fish, nuts and seeds.

# Low-calorie diet

### PROMISE

A low-calorie diet based upon the calorific values of foods, and upon the idea that, if you eat fewer calories than you use, you will burn your body fat as energy and thus lose weight. But the human body is far too complicated to respond to calorie-counting. You can end up on a form of starvation diet yet still fail to shift the pounds.

### OUTCOME

- Food becomes merely the sum of its calorific value, with nutritional value ignored (see pp.32–33). This leads to poor food choices and increased risk of health problems.

- Even essential fats that are vital for optimum health and for weight reduction are labelled as "fattening" and avoided.

- Restricted food intake slows down your metabolism (see pp.26–27), making it hard to sustain any initial weight loss.

- When you return to eating "normally", your metabolism will still be in "famine mode" and so you gain more weight than you originally lost.

# High-protein diet

### PROMISE

A high-protein diet designed to limit your intake of carbohydrates. They usually have an "induction phase" of all-fat and all-protein intake, with carbohydrates to be introduced later in the programme. During this initial phase, weight loss is most noticeable. In practice, many people stay in this induction phase (see p.18), because of the successful short-term weight loss.

### OUTCOME

- Restricted carbohydrate consumption means that you are unlikely to achieve the recommended five portions of fruit and vegetables per day in your dietary intake.

- Long-term use of the induction phase means intake of fibre may be poor, leading to constipation and increasing the risk of colon cancer.

- Poor intake of antioxidants due to lack of fruit and vegetables increases risk of diseases such as cancer, heart disease and arthritis.

- Increased danger of high intake of saturated fats, which may lead to cholesterol problems and thus heighten the risk of heart disease.

# The ultimate shopping list

Keep the following foods, or the majority of them, stocked up in your kitchen and you will easily be able to prepare a healthy Food Doctor meal.

## Grains & wheat

- [ ] Brown rice
- [ ] Buckwheat flour
- [ ] Buckwheat noodles
- [ ] Couscous
- [ ] Gluten-free flour
- [ ] Millet flakes
- [ ] Oats, jumbo
- [ ] Quinoa
- [ ] Rye/wholegrain bread

## Pulses

- [ ] Butter beans, canned
- [ ] Cannellini beans, canned
- [ ] Chick-peas, canned
- [ ] Flageolet beans, canned
- [ ] Lentils, green, red and Puy, canned or dried
- [ ] Mixed beans, canned
- [ ] Mung beans, dried
- [ ] Red kidney beans, canned
- [ ] Split yellow lentils, dried
- [ ] Split yellow peas, dried

## Nuts & seeds

- [ ] Cashew nuts
- [ ] Hazelnuts
- [ ] Linseeds
- [ ] Pine nuts
- [ ] Pumpkin seeds
- [ ] Sesame seeds
- [ ] Sunflower seeds
- [ ] Walnuts

## Herbs

- [ ] Basil
- [ ] Bay leaves
- [ ] Chives
- [ ] Coriander
- [ ] Dill
- [ ] Fennel
- [ ] Lemon grass
- [ ] Marjoram
- [ ] Mint
- [ ] Mixed herbs, dried
- [ ] Oregano, dried
- [ ] Parsley
- [ ] Rosemary
- [ ] Sage
- [ ] Thyme

## Spices

- [ ] Black pepper
- [ ] Caraway seeds
- [ ] Cardamom pods
- [ ] Cayenne
- [ ] Chilli paste
- [ ] Chilli powder
- [ ] Cinnamon, ground
- [ ] Cinnamon, sticks
- [ ] Cloves
- [ ] Coriander seeds
- [ ] Cumin seeds
- [ ] Curry leaves
- [ ] Curry paste (green)
- [ ] Curry powder
- [ ] Fennel seeds
- [ ] Five-spice paste
- [ ] Ginger (fresh)
- [ ] Ginger powder
- [ ] Mango powder
- [ ] Mustard seed (black)
- [ ] Nutmeg
- [ ] Onion powder
- [ ] Paprika, smoked and unsmoked
- [ ] Poppy seeds
- [ ] Star anise
- [ ] Tamarind paste
- [ ] Turmeric

## Oils

- [ ] Avocado oil
- [ ] Olive oil
- [ ] Sesame oil
- [ ] Walnut oil

## Storecupboard essentials

- [ ] Anchovy essence
- [ ] Black olives
- [ ] Carrot juice
- [ ] Coconut, creamed
- [ ] Coconut, milk
- [ ] Honey
- [ ] Horseradish sauce
- [ ] Mixed vegetable juice
- [ ] Mushroom ketchup
- [ ] Mustard, Dijon
- [ ] Mustard, wholegrain
- [ ] Peppers in olive oil
- [ ] Ratatouille, canned
- [ ] Soy sauce
- [ ] Stock, fish
- [ ] Stock, vegetable
- [ ] Stock powder
- [ ] Sun-dried tomatoes in olive oil
- [ ] Tapenade, black
- [ ] Tapenade, green
- [ ] Thai fish sauce
- [ ] Tomato paste
- [ ] Tomatoes, canned
- [ ] Vinegar, balsamic
- [ ] Vinegar, cider
- [ ] Vinegar, white wine
- [ ] White wine
- [ ] Worcestershire sauce

## Fruit

- [ ] Apples
- [ ] Apricots
- [ ] Blackberries
- [ ] Blueberries
- [ ] Grapefruit
- [ ] Kiwi fruit
- [ ] Lemons
- [ ] Limes
- [ ] Oranges
- [ ] Pears
- [ ] Raspberries

## Vegetables

- [ ] Aubergines
- [ ] Avocados
- [ ] Beansprouts
- [ ] Beetroot, baby
- [ ] Broccoli
- [ ] Cabbage, green, red and white
- [ ] Carrots
- [ ] Celeriac
- [ ] Celery
- [ ] Chinese leaves
- [ ] Corn, baby cobs
- [ ] Courgettes
- [ ] Cucumbers
- [ ] Fennel, Florence
- [ ] Garlic
- [ ] Green beans
- [ ] Leeks
- [ ] Lettuce, romaine or cos
- [ ] Mangetout
- [ ] Mixed salad leaves
- [ ] Mushrooms, white and brown
- [ ] Onions, yellow and red
- [ ] Parsnips
- [ ] Peas, frozen
- [ ] Peppers, red, yellow and green
- [ ] Red chillies, fresh
- [ ] Rocket
- [ ] Shallots
- [ ] Spinach
- [ ] Spring onions
- [ ] Sprouted seeds
- [ ] Squash, butternut
- [ ] Sugar snap peas
- [ ] Swedes
- [ ] Sweet potatoes
- [ ] Tomatoes
- [ ] Tomatoes, cherry
- [ ] Watercress

## Dairy

- [ ] Quail's eggs
- [ ] Hen's eggs
- [ ] Feta cheese
- [ ] Goat's cheese (hard)
- [ ] Goat's cheese (soft)
- [ ] Milk
- [ ] Parmesan cheese
- [ ] Quark
- [ ] Tofu, silken (both firm and soft)
- [ ] Yoghurt, live natural

## Meat & fish

- [ ] Anchovy fillets
- [ ] Chicken breasts
- [ ] Chicken, smoked
- [ ] Haddock, smoked
- [ ] Mackerel, smoked
- [ ] Parma ham
- [ ] Prawns, cooked
- [ ] Salmon, fresh fillets
- [ ] Salmon, smoked
- [ ] Scallops
- [ ] Squid
- [ ] Swordfish
- [ ] Tuna, canned
- [ ] Tuna, fresh
- [ ] White fish fillets (cod, haddock etc.)

# The right proportions

You can be as creative as you want about what you eat for breakfast, as long as you stick to The Food Doctor rules about food groups and proportions.

Cup both hands together slightly so that both are showing about 80 per cent of their total surface area. This should give you an indicator for how big your portions should be. Your breakfast should make up about 20 per cent of your daily total food intake.

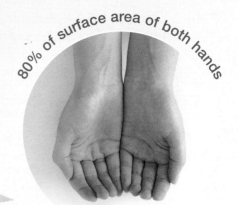

80% of surface area of both hands

**30%** complex starchy carbohydrates

such as oat flakes, sugar-free cereal or wholegrain bread

**40%** protein

such as nuts and seeds, eggs, fish, lean meat, yoghurt or milk

**30%** complex carbohydrates

such as fruit

# Breakfast

The old adage that breakfast is the most important meal of the day couldn't be more true in terms of The Food Doctor plan. Skipping breakfast altogether or eating a high-carbohydrate breakfast is a sure-fire recipe for weight gain.

There is a very good reason why one of my 10 principles recommends not skipping this meal. By eating breakfast you can stimulate the ideal metabolic rate for the day, as long as you make smart food choices. Furthermore, skipping breakfast is likely to set the scene for subsequent highs and lows during the day (see pp.16–17).

## A bad breakfast

A typical breakfast of cereal, black coffee and orange juice contains little fibre, and almost certainly no protein. Since each of these foods falls into one of the categories that encourages an increase in blood-glucose levels and thus triggers insulin production, having a combination of these foods leads to far swifter response, which in turn leaves you feeling hungry sooner than you need to. So, you have a bowl of cereal for breakfast, and are hungry again by the time you get to work, or have finished the school run. Cereals and convenience breakfast foods, which now include branded cereal bars which have a

pleasant aura of health about them, are sugared and refined, with inevitably high GI values (see pp.14–15). However convenient these foods may be, they will not help you lose weight in the long term, so you are going to have to look elsewhere and put a little more effort in this all important first meal of the day.

## A good breakfast

If you like to eat cereal, simply choose a sugar-free cereal, then add some fruit and some protein – perhaps some nuts and seeds. Adding fibre in the form of fruit, and protein in the form of nuts or seeds, while reducing the simple carbohydrate element, changes the breakfast into one that contains 40 per cent protein and fits the portion breakdown (see opposite).

It really doesn't matter whether you want cereal or steak for breakfast, as long as you have the correct food groups in the right ratios. Match your portion size to your hand size, too, and you can start the day any way you like.

### IDEAL CHOICE GRAINS AND BREADS

The breads and grains below are those that have the lowest GI ratings.

| | | | |
|---|---|---|---|
| Wholemeal pasta | 38 | Bulgur wheat | 48 |
| Rye bread | 41 | Sourdough rye | 48 |
| Pumpernickel | 41 | Brown rice | 50 |
| Oatmeal | 42 | Wholegrain bread | 51 |
| Toasted muesli | 43 | Multigrain porridge | 55 |

### POOR CHOICE GRAINS AND BREADS

Avoid refined options such as those below, as they are low in fibre and have high GI ratings.

| | | | |
|---|---|---|---|
| Corn flakes | 85 | Bagel | 72 |
| White bread | 78 | Crumpet | 69 |
| English muffin | 77 | Croissant | 67 |
| Cocoa puffs | 77 | Durum wheat pasta | 61 |
| Waffles | 76 | White rice | 60 |

# Menu ideas

# Quick breakfasts

Browse these ideas for inspiration on how to create a perfectly balanced, nutritious and tasty breakfast. They are quick to make, so perfect for a rushed weekday morning.

## Fruit smoothie

- **fruit** two palmfuls of any fruit, such as strawberries, blackberries, raspberries, plums, apricots, peaches, nectarines or mangoes

and

- **yoghurt** a couple of tablespoons of live natural low-fat yoghurt

and

- **seeds** about a tablespoon of seeds, such as linseeds or sunflower seeds

and

- **full-fat milk** enough milk to create the right consistency

## Quick classic cereal

- **cereal** about 4 tablespoons of cereal, such as plain (unsweetened) corn flakes, bran flakes or barley flakes

and

- **nuts** a small palmful of mixed nuts, such as Brazil nuts, pecans, walnuts, hazelnuts and almonds

and

- **full-fat milk** a little more than enough milk to moisten the cereal: choose from cow's milk, goat's milk, sheep's milk, unsweetened rice milk or unsweetened soya milk

## Nut butter on toast

- **toast** 2 thin slices of toast, made from pumpernickel, wholemeal or rye bread

and

- **sugar-free nut butter** a thin coating of either cashew, peanut or almond butter

Yoghurt with fruit and seeds

Fruit smoothie

Quick classic cereal

## Cheese or ham with bread

- **bread** 2 slices of bread, such as rye, wholemeal or pumpernickel

  and

- **cheese** a few thin slices of any hard cheese, such as cheddar or hard goat's cheese

  or

- **meat** a few slices of lean meat, such as chicken, turkey or ham (not honey-roast or sweet-cure)

## Yoghurt with fruit and seeds

- **yoghurt** about 2–3 tablespoons of live natural low-fat yoghurt

  and

- **fruits** a large palmful of any chopped fruit, such as apples or pears, or whole cranberries, blackberries, raspberries or blueberries

  and

- **nuts and seeds** a tablespoon of any combination of nuts and seeds, such as flaked almonds, chopped hazelnuts or walnuts, and linseeds, sunflower or pumpkin seeds

## Eggs with toast or crackers

- **eggs** two eggs poached, scrambled or soft-boiled

  and

- **toast or crackers** a thick slice of toast, made from pumpernickel, wholemeal or rye bread, or a couple of crispbreads, oatcakes or rice cakes

# Menu ideas

# Leisurely breakfasts

Sometimes, especially at the weekend, breakfast can be a more indulgent affair. These recipes are still quick and not too involved, but are more of a treat than an everyday event.

## Sweet pancake

- **basic pancake wrap** one pancake wrap (*see p.104*)

and

- **fruit** a palmful of chopped fruit, such as apples, pears, peaches, nectarines, plums, kiwifruit, papaya and mangoes

and

- **yoghurt** a couple of tablespoons of live natural low-fat yoghurt

and

- **nuts** a tablespoon of chopped nuts, such as walnuts and hazelnuts

## Fish-topped toast

- **fish** one serving of oily fish, such as kippers, mackerel or sardines, chopped or mashed very roughly

and

- **tomato** one chopped tomato, or a chopped roasted red pepper, mixed in with the fish

and

- **toast** one slice of toast, made from pumpernickel, wholemeal or rye bread

## Eggs with wilted spinach

- **eggs** two eggs, poached, scrambled or soft-boiled

and

- **spinach** a generous handful of wilted spinach or other steamed or grilled vegetables, such as pak choi, kale or asparagus

Frittata

Fruit salad

Smoked salmon pancake

## Fruit salad

- **fruit** a palmful of fruit, such as blackberries, strawberries, blueberries, raspberries, red- and blackcurrants, apples, pears, plums and mangoes

  and

- **yoghurt** a couple of tablespoons of live natural low-fat yoghurt

  and

- **nuts and seeds** a tablespoon of mixed chopped nuts and seeds, such as Brazil nuts, almonds, sunflower seeds and linseeds

## Frittata

- **frittata** choose from recipes such as leek, Mediterranean, mushroom and tomato, red pesto or sweet potato and dill (*see pp.58, 86 and 87*), or make your own recipe with ingredients you have available, such as olives, goat's cheese and anchovies, or smoked mackerel, onion and sweetcorn

  and

- **toast** one slice of toast, made from pumpernickel, wholemeal or rye bread, with a thin scraping of butter if you wish

## Savoury pancake

- **basic pancake wrap** one pancake wrap (*see p.104*)

  and

- **egg and smoked salmon** one poached or scrambled egg and a few pieces of smoked salmon

  or

- **goat's cheese** a palm-sized portion of hard or soft goat's cheese with some rocket leaves or a chopped baked tomato

# Millet porridge

A pear instead of the apple would be equally good with this satisfying porridge. If you don't have any millet, alternative cereals that work equally well are suggested. Serves two.

ready in **15** minutes

75g (2½oz) millet flakes (or barley flakes or buckwheat flakes)

300ml (½ pint) water

4 tablespoons live natural yoghurt

1 large crunchy apple, cored but not peeled, and sliced or grated

2 tablespoons pumpkin seeds

Place the millet flakes and water in a small saucepan, mix together and bring to boiling point. Quickly reduce to a simmer and cook the mixture gently for 5–10 minutes, until all the water is absorbed and a soft porridge results.

Stir in the yoghurt to make a creamy porridge, then divide between two bowls. Top each with the apple and the pumpkin seeds and serve immediately.

# Sunshine smoothie and oatcakes

This smoothie is a wonderful colour and rich in beta-carotene and vitamin C. The ingredients make about 700ml (nearly 1¼ pints), enough to serve two people at breakfast and with some left over for a mid-morning snack.

**ready in 10 minutes**

4 fresh apricots, halved and stoned

1 mango, halved, stoned and flesh cut into chunks

Juice of 2 oranges (approx. 100ml/3½fl oz)

200ml (7fl oz) carrot juice

2 tablespoons linseeds

Put the apricots, mango, juices and linseeds in a blender and blend until the mixture is smooth and the linseeds are broken up. (For a really smooth version, grind the linseeds before putting them in the blender.) Drink 200ml (7fl oz) for breakfast, with two oatcakes per person spread with low-fat cottage cheese or quark to provide protein.

Note: The remainder of the smoothie can be used for a quick snack during the morning. If it is too thick, just blend with 100g (3½oz) silken tofu and add some more carrot juice.

# Mushroom and tomato frittata

This slow-cooked omelette makes an excellent weekend breakfast dish. Teamed with a green salad it also works well as a main meal. Serves two.

ready in **10** minutes

1 tablespoon olive oil

Approx. 75g (2½oz) brown mushrooms, sliced

4 eggs

2 tablespoons live natural yoghurt

Freshly ground black pepper

1–2 tablespoons chopped parsley

2 medium tomatoes, chopped

Heat the olive oil in an omelette pan, add the mushrooms and soften over a gentle heat.

Break the eggs into a bowl, beat them lightly and add the yoghurt, black pepper, and chopped parsley. Mix well, then stir in the chopped tomatoes.

Pour the mixture over the mushrooms in the pan, spreading the filling evenly over the base. Cook over a gentle heat until the bottom of the omelette is firm.

To cook the top you can either slide the whole pan under a hot grill for a couple of minutes or slide the frittata on to a plate, invert and place back into the pan. Divide the frittata in two and serve with rye or wholemeal bread.

# Smoked salmon and poached egg pancake

These luxurious egg and salmon wraps are a great way to start the day. Experiment with other fillings, too, such as goat's cheese and rocket or scrambled egg with spinach. Serves two.

ready in **10** minutes

2 eggs

2 pancake wraps (*see p.104 for basic pancake wrap*)

2 slices smoked salmon (approx. 60g/2oz total weight)

Juice of ½ lemon

Fill a pan with water, add a dash of vinegar, and bring it to the boil. Break each egg into a saucer and slide them into the boiling water. Return the water to the boil, and poach the eggs until they are firmly set, but not hard. Remove the eggs with a slotted spoon and set aside.

Heat a small frying pan or omelette pan and add a little olive oil. If the pancakes are already cooked, heat them one at a time in the pan on both sides. If you are cooking the pancakes fresh, cook one side, flip over.

While you are still cooking/heating the second side, place a slice of smoked salmon on one half of the pancake, squeeze over the lemon juice, and slide an egg on top. Fold the pancake in half over the filling and set aside while you repeat for the second pancake. Serve at once.

# The right proportions

A snack simply needs to be a combination of protein and carbohydrates. It doesn't have to be complicated or time-consuming. It's up to you to be imaginative and find protein and carbohydrate combinations that you like.

Use one hand, slightly cupped so that it is showing about 80 per cent of its surface area, as an indicator for how big your portion size should be. Your mid-morning and mid-afternoon snack should each make up about 10 per cent of your daily total food intake.

**80% of one hand surface area**

**40%** protein
such as the pulses in this houmous, nuts and seeds, eggs, fish or lean meat

**60%** complex carbohydrates
such as fruit or vegetables

# Snacks

The Food Doctor plan relies upon a number of principles, and eating little and often is one of the most important of these. Fuelling up frequently keeps the metabolism ticking over evenly and supplies you with a steady energy supply.

Many clients come from a "three square meals a day" background and are nervous about eating between meals. They worry that if they eat five times a day they will eat far too much – a concern that stems from a history of denial and excess. With The Food Doctor plan, however, the danger of over-eating is reduced as you will be eating exactly the same amount as you would with the traditional three meals a day, but dividing them into five smaller meals (*see pp.28–29*).

## Avoid the insulin rollercoaster

Eating mid-morning and mid-afternoon is vital to keep your energy levels constant and avoid the "lows" leading to cravings and poor food choices. When you're hungry, for example, rather than drink coffee, which will raise blood-glucose levels and suppress the normal hunger response, you could have a simple snack that will supply nutrients and slow-releasing energy instead. It doesn't have to be complicated, nor does it have to be traditional or hard work (*see pp.62–65 for suggestions*).

Snacks can be as simple as a cracker or two with unsweetened nut butter, or a piece of fibrous fruit, such as an apple or pear, with some nuts or mixed seeds. Eating a small palmful of seeds with a piece of fruit will supply minerals, nutrients, essential fats and protein, while the fruit offers fibre and yet more nutrients. Perhaps of more relevance to weight loss, the combination of protein, essential fats and fibre is one that is broken down slowly by the body so you will limit hunger, and let blood-glucose levels rise gently to avoid triggering a surge of insulin.

Pre-made foods from the deli counter can make ideal bases for good snacks, such as houmous with some celery or a carrot. It doesn't have to be beautiful, you don't need plates, no tables need laying – you just open the tub of houmous and scoop some up with the vegetables. Left-overs also make great snacks (*see pp.36–37*). For example, if you have some chicken and vegetables for a main meal, make a little more and leave it for snack-time.

### IDEAL FRUIT CHOICES
These fruits make great snack choices as they have a low GI rating.

| | | | |
|---|---|---|---|
| Apricots | 20 | Peaches | 30 |
| Grapefruit | 20 | Strawberries | 32 |
| Cherries | 22 | Pears | 35 |
| Plums | 22 | Oranges | 35 |
| Apples | 30 | Figs (fresh) | 35 |

### POOR FRUIT CHOICES
Their quick conversion into sugar and high GI rating make these fruits poor choices.

| | | | |
|---|---|---|---|
| Watermelon | 72 | Bananas | 65 |
| Mixed dried fruit | 70 | Figs (dried) | 61 |
| Pineapple | 66 | Black grapes | 59 |
| Cantaloupe melon | 65 | Kiwifruit | 58 |
| Raisins | 65 | Orange juice | 57 |

# Menu ideas

# Snacks to pack

Often the key to a healthy snack is convenience. They must be both simple to make and practical to pack. These snacks are ready in minutes but stave off hunger for much longer.

## Fruit and nuts

- **fruit** a piece of fruit, such as an apple, pear, peach or nectarine, or a couple of apricots, plums, clementines or mandarin oranges, or a palmful of grapes or berries

  and

- **nuts** five or six nuts, such as almonds, walnuts, hazelnuts, pecans or Brazil nuts

## Houmous with crudités

- **houmous** a tablespoon of houmous, preferably home-made

  and

- **vegetable crudités** a handful of raw chopped vegetables, such as carrots, celery, cucumber, cauliflower and broccoli florets, cherry tomatoes, spring onions, or red, green, yellow or orange peppers

## Mash toppers

- **mash** a tablespoon of of mash, such as sweet potato and goat's cheese, mushroom, tapenade and tofu or butter bean and mustard (*see pp.66–67 for recipes*)

  and

- **toast or crackers** a couple of thin slices of toast made from wholemeal or rye bread, or two crackers, such as crispbreads, oatcakes or rice cakes

Fruit and nuts

Topped rice cakes

Houmous with crudités

## Crackers with nut butter

- **crackers**  two crackers, such as crispbreads, oatcakes or rice cakes

  and

- **sugar-free nut butter**  a thin coating of either cashew, peanut or almond butter

## Yoghurt and fruit

- **yoghurt**  a small pot of live natural low-fat yoghurt

  and

- **fruit**  a palmful of soft berries stirred into your yoghurt, such as strawberries, raspberries or blackberries, or some chopped fruit, such as apricot, mango, plum, papaya, nectarine, apple or pear

  and

- **seeds**  a sprinkling of seeds, such as sunflower, pumpkin or linseeds

## Topped rice cakes

- **dip or spread**  a tablespoon of your choice of dip, preferably home-made (for a selection of dips such as fish, avocado or pepper and sun-dried tomato, *see pp.68–69*)

  and

- **rice cakes**  two rice cakes or other crackers, such as crispbreads or oatcakes

# Quick and easy snacks ...

Snacks keep the body supplied with a steady energy supply. If you snack regularly, you'll be less likely to over-eat at meal-times or make poor food choices due to hunger.

## The usual choice

**Dried fruits and an "energy bar"** I can almost sense your disappointment at being told this isn't a perfect choice as it might seem very healthy. There are still a few substitutions you could make, however, to turn this into a truly healthy snack.

**Bread and cheese** Many of us find it hard to resist a chunk of fresh bread and cheese: with a few careful substitutions The Food Doctor Everyday Diet allows you to continue enjoying such pleasures, while still controlling your weight.

**Low-fat biscuits** Surely dieters can eat biscuits if they are labelled low in fat? Unfortunately not. To create flavour, low-fat options are often packed full of sugar and sweeteners, guaranteed to trigger insulin production. However convenient this option seems, there is always a price to pay.

# and how to improve them

## The Food Doctor choice

Many energy bars are packed with sugars and cheap ingredients instead of the nuts and seeds required to supply protein. Dried fruits are a poor-choice carbohydrate as they have a high GI rating.

- Choose fresh fruits that have low GI scores, such as apples, plums, pears or apricots.
- Instead of an energy bar, eat five or six hazelnuts or other nuts with your piece of fruit.
- As a tasty alternative protein source to nuts, try a handful of mixed sunflower and pumpkin seeds.

White bread is a poor choice as it is low in fibre and has a high GI value. Instead, try rye bread or oatcakes as this allows you to vary your grain intake, or sourdough if you want to avoid yeast.

- Cottage cheese, possibly flavoured with some fresh herbs or spring onions, makes a tangy alternative topping.
- Goat's cheese is relatively low in fat and makes a good substitute for cow's-milk cheeses.
- Avoid blue and aged cheeses because they contain mould that can lead to excess yeast formation in the intestines.

If convenience is the key, try to avoid the sweet biscuit section of a shop and buy some oatcakes instead. They are just as easy to eat on the go. Team them with some protein for the ideal snack.

- The quickest accompaniment to your crackers is to layer some lean ham on top.
- Houmous is a great protein option. If you have time, make it yourself so it's additive-free.
- Chopped cucumber mixed with linseeds, mint and natural yoghurt makes a healthy topping.

# Mash toppers

These mashes are easy to make, filling and wonderfully versatile. Spread on rice-cakes, oatcakes or a piece of rye bread, they make deliciously wholesome snacks. A spoonful of your favourite mash can also spice up a lunch or dinner, just add it on the side or as a topping.

## Pea, ginger and tapenade mash

ready in **15** minutes

150g (5oz) frozen peas, thawed

1cm (½in) piece fresh root ginger, peeled and finely grated

2 tablespoons olive oil

Juice of ½ orange

Grated zest of ½ orange

Grated zest of ½ lemon

2 spring onions, finely chopped

1 garlic clove, finely chopped

60g (2oz) tofu (silken, preferably)

5 teaspoons green tapenade (*see p.148*)

Juice of ½ lemon

Freshly ground black pepper

Live natural yoghurt (optional)

1 tablespoon chopped fresh mint

Put the peas, ginger, olive oil, orange juice, zests, spring onions and garlic in a heavy-based pan. Bring to the boil, reduce the heat and simmer gently for 10 minutes, until the peas are well cooked.

Pour the mixture into a blender, add the tofu and blend to make a slightly rough mash. Alternatively, add the tofu to the pan and mash it. Turn the mash into a bowl and stir in the tapenade, lemon juice and black pepper to taste. If the mash seems too thick, stir in a little more olive oil and/or some yoghurt. Finally, stir in the mint.

## Sweet potato and goat's cheese mash

ready in **30** minutes

200g (7oz) sweet potato, peeled and coarsely chopped

1 tablespoon olive oil

2 garlic cloves in their skins, tips chopped off

75g (2½oz) soft goat's cheese (a "log" is excellent), roughly cubed

Lemon juice, to taste

Freshly ground black pepper

1–2 tablespoons finely chopped fresh coriander

Preheat the oven to 350°C/180°F/ gas mark 4.

Put the chopped sweet potato in a baking dish with the olive oil and garlic cloves. Cover the dish and put it in the preheated oven. Bake for about 25 minutes, or until the sweet potato pieces are soft.

Squeeze the soft garlic out of their skins and tip into a bowl with the sweet potato. Add the goat's cheese and mash everything together until well blended, but not reduced to a smooth purée. Add lemon juice and pepper to taste and plenty of chopped coriander.

Red lentils cumin and turmeric mash

Butter bean and mustard mash

Mushroom, tapenade and tofu mash

Pea, ginger and green tapenade mash

# Red lentils, cumin and turmeric mash

**ready in 25 minutes**

1 tablespoon olive oil

1 onion (approx. 200g/7oz), finely chopped

1 garlic clove, chopped

1 bay leaf

2 teaspoons turmeric

2 teaspoons curry powder

½ teaspoon chilli paste

2 teaspoons black mustard seeds

½ teaspoon cumin seeds

1 x approx. 400g/13oz can red lentils, drained and rinsed

300ml (½ pint) vegetable stock (*see p.149*)

1–2 tablespoons finely chopped fresh coriander

Freshly ground black pepper

Heat the olive oil in a heavy-based saucepan and add the onion, garlic and bay leaf. Cook gently until the onion is soft but not coloured.

Stir in the turmeric, curry powder, chilli paste, mustard seeds and cumin and continue cooking gently for 3–4 minutes to allow the onion to absorb the flavours. Add the lentils and the stock. Stir, bring to the boil, reduce the heat and simmer very gently for about 15 minutes, until the lentils are very tender and the stock absorbed.

When cooking is complete, leave the lentils in the pan to cool a little then mash them very coarsely. Stir in the coriander and black pepper.

# Butter bean and mustard mash

**ready in 20 minutes**

1 x approx. 400g (13oz) can butter beans, drained and rinsed

Approx. 300ml (½ pint) vegetable stock (*see p.149*)

2 tablespoons olive oil

1 heaped teaspoon Dijon mustard

2–3 tablespoons chopped parsley

Freshly ground black pepper

Put the beans in a heavy-based saucepan and pour in enough vegetable stock to cover. Bring to the boil, cover the pan, reduce the heat and simmer for about 15–20 minutes, until the beans have softened. Drain, reserving the stock.

Put the hot beans in a bowl and add the olive oil and mustard. Mash the mixture with a fork or a potato masher until it is quite smooth. Stir in the chopped parsley and more olive oil, if necessary, to loosen the mixture. If the mash still seems too stiff, stir in a little of the reserved stock.

# Mushroom, tapenade & tofu mash

**ready in 15 minutes**

2 tablespoons olive oil

½ onion (approx. 60g/2oz), very finely chopped

50g (2oz) tofu (preferably silken), very finely chopped

150g (5oz) well-flavoured mushrooms, such as brown mushrooms, field mushrooms, exotic mushrooms, or a mixture

2 rounded teaspoons black olive tapenade (*see p.148*)

Juice of ½ lemon

Freshly ground black pepper

1 tablespoon snipped chives

Heat the oil in a heavy-based saucepan, add the onion and cook until the onion is softened but not coloured. Add the tofu and cook, stirring, for 2–3 minutes. Add the mushrooms, stir well and allow to cook gently for about 5 minutes, or until the mushrooms are soft. Stir in the tapenade, lemon juice and some black pepper. Add the chives.

**SERVING IDEAS**

**For a snack** Spread on two rice-cakes or oatcakes as a perfect snack.

**For lunch** Use as a filling for a small jacket potato with a dressed green salad on the side.

**For dinner** Thin with a little olive oil or live natural yoghurt to make a sauce for grilled fish or chicken.

# Dips and sauces

A great way of using up left-overs, these recipes can be served cold as a dip with crudités or as a topping for rice cakes or crackers, but can also be used to liven up a main meal. The avocado and fish dips will only keep for one day, but the others will last 4–5 days in an airtight container in the fridge.

---

### SERVING IDEAS

**For a snack** These recipes all work well on a rice cake or can be used as a tasty dip.

**For lunch** Red pesto or pepper and sun-dried tomato sauce make great pasta sauces tossed with some feta or chicken pieces.

**For dinner** Try the pepper and sun-dried tomato sauce hot with grilled fish or a stir-fry.

---

## Fish dip

ready in **5** minutes

60g (2oz) cold cooked fish

2 tablespoons Quark or other low-fat cream cheese

2 tablespoons lemon juice

¼ teaspoon anchovy essence (or ¼ teaspoon of either anchovy paste or Thai fish sauce)

1 tablespoon finely chopped fresh dill

Put all the ingredients in a bowl and mash them roughly together with a fork.

Fish dip

Avocado dip

Red pesto

# Avocado dip

ready in **5** minutes

½ avocado, stoned, peeled and roughly chopped

1 tablespoon lime juice

½ teaspoon grated fresh root ginger

2 tablespoons live natural yoghurt

1 tablespoon finely chopped coriander

Put all the ingredients in a bowl and mash well with a fork. Top with some pine nuts for a little additional protein.

# Red pesto

ready in **10** minutes

1 small jar (approx. 250g/8oz) sun-dried tomatoes in oil, drained and chopped

125g (4oz) pine nuts

150ml (¼ pint) olive oil

Juice of ½ lemon

1 garlic clove

Freshly ground black pepper

Leaves from a small bunch parsley

Place all the ingredients in a blender or food processor and blend until fairly smooth.

# Pepper and sun-dried tomato sauce

ready in **10** minutes

1 x approx. 250g (8oz) jar mixed peppers

1 x approx. 250g (8oz) jar sun-dried tomatoes in oil

5 tablespoons olive oil

Juice of ½ lemon

Freshly ground black pepper

Drain the peppers and sun-dried tomatoes and put them in a blender. Add the oil and lemon juice and blend until the mixture is thick but not too smooth. Scrape into a bowl, add black pepper to taste.

# Butter beans with pepper and sun-dried tomato sauce

ready in **15** minutes

1 tablespoon olive oil

1 garlic clove, crushed

4 tablespoons pepper and sun-dried tomato sauce (*see above*)

100 ml (3½fl oz) water

1 x approx. 400g (13oz) can butter beans, drained and rinsed

Heat the oil in a small, heavy-based saucepan. Add the garlic and cook for a minute or two to release its flavour. Add the pepper sauce and water, then the beans. Increase the temperature and simmer the ingredients for about 5 minutes, until the sauce is thick and the beans have heated through.

Pepper and sun-dried tomato sauce

# Lunch – the right proportions

Lunch can be a fresh cold salad prepared in minutes or a delicious cooked dish – as long as the food-group proportions fit the profile outlined below.

Cup both hands together with palms and fingers opened out showing 100 per cent of their total surface area. This should give you an indication of how big your portion size should be. Your lunch should make up about 30 per cent of your daily total food intake.

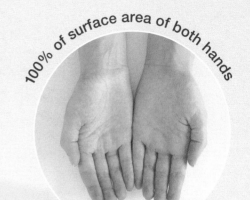

100% of surface area of both hands

40% complex carbohydrates
such as green vegetables

20%
complex starchy
carbohydrates
such as brown rice,
wholegrain bread,
wholewheat pasta
or potatoes

40% protein
such as fish, chicken,
tofu or pulses

# Lunch and dinner

Serial dieters will know all too well that main meals can be an area fraught with difficulty. There is a general fear of over-eating, but following The Food Doctor plan helps prepare you for main meals by ensuring that you are not overly hungry when you eat, and by giving you a clear idea of portion size too.

The ratios for protein and complex carbohydrates for lunch and dinner (*see opposite and overleaf*) are both 40:60, although for lunch 20 per cent of those complex carbohydrates are from starchy sources such as potatoes or brown rice. Use your hands as a simple guide to the size of the protein portion: it is just under one "hand's-worth" (40 per cent of the total surface area of both hands).

## A perfect lunch

Lunch is often eaten at work or at home between commitments or appointments. It doesn't have to be time-consuming, however (*see pp.36–37*). Making extra food the night before is my first choice for a convenient lunch. If you cooked at home the previous evening, simply make enough to take to work or leave in the fridge for next day's lunch. If you haven't got any leftovers, then just make sure you have some basic ingredients available to throw together – see my suggestions for recipes and menus (*see pp.76–77, 82–83*).

If you have a sandwich, choose one that has a complete protein filling, such as tuna, prawns, chicken or turkey. Sandwiches are by their nature higher in carbohydrates than I would ideally like you to have, but if you take a look at pages 82–83 you can see how easy it is to make them into more appropriate bases for an ideal Food Doctor meal. You aren't obliged to eat the sandwich alone, either: if you feel that it is lacking in protein, then you could add a palmful of mixed nuts and seeds to redress the balance.

Many shops offer boxed salads, which are a great base for lunch. Often the protein is lacking, however, so if you get a pre-made tuna salad, then perhaps buy a small extra can of tuna as well and add it in.

If possible, don't buy lunch out every day as you won't have the same level of control that you have if you make something yourself. Once again, however, this doesn't mean complicated menus or hard work. You could do something as

---

### IDEAL PROTEIN CHOICES

These complete proteins are low in saturated fats and some contain beneficial essential fatty acids.

| | |
|---|---|
| Chicken (skinless) | Quorn |
| Eggs | Seeds |
| Fish (especially oily fish) | Tofu |
| Nuts (raw) | Turkey (skinless) |
| Pulses | Veal |

### POOR PROTEIN CHOICES

Since these proteins are potential sources of trans or saturated fats, they are not ideal choices.

| | |
|---|---|
| Bacon | Lamb |
| Beef | Pheasant |
| Duck | Salami |
| Goose | Sausages |
| Ham | Soft cheese |

simple as open a can of sardines, chop in some fresh dill or parsley, and eat the mixture with a chopped pepper, a few salad leaves and a slice of wholemeal bread. Your meal doesn't have to be complicated or time-consuming to prepare – have whatever you feel like eating, as long as you keep the food group ratios in mind.

On the assumption that you ate breakfast at around 8am and a snack around 10.30am or so, lunch will probably be around 1pm. I do suggest that you try and eat earlier rather than later. This will help you make better food decisions and not leave you in a position where your blood-glucose levels are very low, which will lead to hunger and cravings. Eating later makes you more likely to make poor food choices. The same applies in the evening: aim to eat at about 7–7.30pm if possible, having had a mid-afternoon snack at approximately 4pm.

## Dinner-time

When it comes to preparing an evening meal, all too often clients tell me "I don't have time" or "I don't get in until late". I am sympathetic to the time issue – I work long hours too – but in order to achieve your goals you must look at the importance you have given to food in the past. If you usually rely on ready-made meals – the heat-and-eat sort of thing – then you must ask yourself how much this has played a part in your weight gain. Most ready-made meals have far higher fat and sugar levels than you might expect

and also, as protein usually costs more than carbohydrates, the meal costs are minimised if protein is limited.

When I discuss cooking with clients, I think there is a misconception that it requires a huge amount of time, and that's simply not the case. If you look at the recipes in this book you will see that many take just ten minutes to prepare, and others only a little longer. There is minimal effort in most of them, and I have tried to ensure that they are more like assembling or preparing food rather than "serious" cooking.

Occasionally I hear from clients that The Food Doctor plan for the evening meal doesn't quite satisfy them: if so, I suggest that, rather than eating more at dinner, or eating something sweet and sugary afterwards, take a break of an hour or so, and then have a very small snack, once again with protein and vegetables. This could be some crudités and dip, or tuna with some lettuce leaves. It may not be traditional, but it works, and encourages sustainable and healthy weight loss.

## What to drink with your meal

I love wine. Drinking a glass or two at dinner is a real pleasure, and alcohol is not forbidden on The Food Doctor plan as long as you follow the rules (*see p.145*). If you choose not to drink alcohol, avoid juices and colas as they are sweetened and caffeinated. Water is best, whether sparkling or still, plain or flavoured with a slice of lemon, lime or whatever you fancy, as long as it's sugar-free.

---

### IDEAL VEGETABLE CHOICES

There are so many good vegetable choices, but these ones have some of the lowest GI values.

| | | | |
|---|---|---|---|
| Aubergines | 10 | Onions | 10 |
| Broccoli | 10 | Red peppers | 10 |
| Cabbage | 10 | Spinach | 10 |
| Lettuce | 10 | Tomatoes | 10 |
| Mushrooms | 10 | Carrots (raw) | 35 |

### POOR VEGETABLE CHOICES

Their high GI ratings make these vegetables relatively poor choices for your meal.

| | | | |
|---|---|---|---|
| Parsnips | 97 | Pumpkin | 75 |
| Potatoes (chips) | 95 | Turnips | 70 |
| Potatoes (mashed) | 90 | Potatoes (baked) | 65 |
| Carrots (cooked) | 85 | Beetroot | 64 |
| Broad beans | 80 | Potatoes (boiled) | 62 |

# Dinner – the right proportions

For your evening meal, 60 per cent of your meal should be based on vegetables but, unlike at lunch-time, you should avoid starchy complex carbohydrates such as grains and potatoes.

Cup both hands together with your palms and fingers opened out showing 100 per cent of their total surface area. This will give you an indication of how big your portion size should be. Your evening meal should make up about 30 per cent of your daily total food intake.

100% of surface area of both hands

**40%**
protein
such as eggs, fish, tofu, pulses or lean meat

**60%** complex carbohydrates
such as a selection of vegetables

# Menu ideas

# Lunch or dinner

Although your lunch and dinner will be about the same size, the proportions of the food groups will differ slightly. These ideas show you how easy it is to adapt the ratios to suit.

## Chicken

- **chicken**  one portion of a simple chicken dish such as Cajun-spiced chicken or Indian spicy chicken (*see pp.130–31*), or chicken in summer herbs (*see p.123*) or coconut chicken (*see p.84*)

and

- **for lunch**  serve with a small jacket potato or few new potatoes, and a small portion of steamed green vegetables

or

- **for dinner**  serve with a large portion of steamed green vegetables

## Eggs

- **eggs**  two eggs cooked as an omelette or a frittata, for example – either simply seasoned or cooked with a delicious filling (*see pp.58, 86–87, 140*)

and

- **for lunch**  serve with a chunk of wholemeal bread and a plain salad of green leaves or a mixed side-salad (*see pp.112–13*)

or

- **for dinner**  serve with a large portion of side-salad, or a large salad of leaves and tomatoes

## Soup

- **soup**  one portion of (preferably home-made) soup, such as prawn and watercress (*see p.101*) or vegetable and bean (*see p.103*)

and

- **for lunch**  serve with some wholemeal bread and perhaps a green salad

or

- **for dinner**  add extra vegetables to the soup or serve with a side-salad

Salmon

Chick-pea and ratatouille stew

Prawn and sweet chilli stir-fry

## Fish

- **fish**  one portion of grilled or poached fish, such as salmon or plaice, or a portion of a recipe such as seared cod (*see p.89*), prawn and sweet chilli stir-fry (*see p.108*) or swordfish with coriander and lime (*see p.98*)

and

- **for lunch**  serve with a portion of brown rice or a few new potatoes, and a small portion of grilled vegetables

or

- **for dinner**  serve with a large portion of grilled vegetables over a mixed leaf salad: drizzle over a tangy dressing (*see pp.128–29*)

## Pulses

- **pulses**  one portion of a pulse-based dish, such as feta, tomato and bean stir-fry (*see p.109*), chick-pea and ratatouille stew (*see p.137*) or butter beans Italian-style (*see p.132*)

and

- **for lunch**  serve with buckwheat noodles or brown rice

or

- **for dinner**  increase the proportion of complex carbohydrates a little by adding a few extra vegetables to your dish

## Tofu

- **tofu**  one portion of any tofu dish, such as leeks in red pesto and tofu sauce (*see p.106*) or green and white salad (*see p.113*)

and

- **for lunch**  serve with brown rice and steamed green vegetables

or

- **for dinner**  serve with a large portion of steamed green vegetables

# Menu ideas

# Packed lunches

Many of us do not have access to a kitchen during the day, so lunch needs to be either prepared in advance or very simple to assemble. Here are some ideas.

## Cheese salad

- **cheese**  a palm-sized portion of cheese, such as mozzarella, cottage cheese, feta or goat's cheese

and

- **salad**  a mixture of any fresh salad ingredients, such as a large handful of leaves, half an avocado, a carrot, and a few olives with a dressing (*see pp.114–15*)

and

- **bread**  one large slice of bread, such as wholemeal, granary, rye or gluten-free bread

## Healthy sandwich

- **protein filling**  a protein-based filling such as one sliced egg flavoured with herbs and black pepper, a large tablespoon of cottage cheese, or a palm-sized portion of goat's cheese, chicken, turkey, ham or smoked salmon

and

- **salad**  a handful of salad leaves and a few slices of tomato

and

- **bread**  two thin slices of bread, such as rye, wholemeal, granary or gluten-free bread

## Rice salad with chicken

- **chicken**  a palm-sized portion of grilled chicken (perhaps left-overs from the previous night's meal or a barbecue)

and

- **rice salad**  a few tablespoons of brown rice mixed with a dressing (*see pp.114–15*) and two tablespoons of grilled vegetables, such as asparagus, broccoli, leek or string beans, or an equivalent amount of raw chopped vegetables such as tomatoes, cucumber, red peppers and spring onions

Healthy sandwich

Crackers with topping

Soup

## Crackers with topping

■ **topping** any protein-based topping, such as two boiled eggs chopped with mixed herbs, cottage cheese with chopped spring onion and cucumber, or fish topping (*see pp.37, 68*)

and

■ **crackers** two crackers, such as rice cakes, oatcakes or crispbreads

and

■ **vegetables** a few cherry tomatoes, for example, or some carrot, sweet pepper or cucumber strips

## Pasta salad

■ **fish** a palm-sized portion of fish, such as smoked mackerel or canned tuna, salmon or mackerel

and

■ **pasta** a small portion of wholewheat, buckwheat or corn pasta

and

■ **salad vegetables** a large palmful of mixed vegetables, such as a spring onion, a small sweet pepper, two tomatoes, two mushrooms and a quarter of a courgette

## Soup with fresh bread

■ **soup** one portion of (preferably home-made) soup, such as smoked fish chowder (*see p.85*), tomato and red pepper soup with cannellini beans (*see p.99*) or very quick gazpacho (*see p.101*)

and

■ **bread** one thick slice of bread, such as wholemeal, granary, rye or gluten-free bread

# Menu ideas

# Quick meals

Possibly the most common excuse I hear is that eating healthily takes too much time. Here are six great ideas to dispel that myth. Start experimenting by varying the ingredients.

## Stir-fry

- **protein**  one portion of chicken, turkey or fish, cut into strips, or prawns, tofu cubes or pulses: if you wish, you could follow a stir-fry recipe such as chicken and cashew (*see p.102*) or feta, tomato and bean (*see p.109*)

  and

- **vegetables**  if you're not following one of the recipes above, add a large handful of mixed chopped vegetables to your protein choice, such as pak choi, spinach, sweet peppers, mangetout, mushrooms and beansprouts

  and (if lunch-time)

- **noodles**  a small portion of buckwheat noodles

## Frittata with green leaves

- **frittata**  choose from one of my frittata recipes, such as mushroom and tomato (*see p.58*), leek, Mediterranean, red pesto and sweet potato and dill (*see pp.86–87*)

  and

- **green leaves**  a generous handful of mixed salad leaves, such as watercress, rocket, red chard, baby spinach and lamb's lettuce

  and (if lunch-time)

- **jacket potato**  one small baked potato

## Salmon with steamed vegetables

- **salmon**  one fillet simply poached or grilled, livened up with a marinade such as yoghurt and ginger (*see p.127*) or cooked according to a recipe such as lime and dill salmon or coconut and coriander salmon (*see p.124–25*)

  and

- **vegetables**  a large portion of steamed vegetables, such as broccoli, cauliflower, mangetout, green beans, kale, spinach, asparagus, Savoy cabbage, carrots and baby corn cobs

Sprouted seed salad

Chicken and cashew stir-fry

Cinnamon seared tuna

## Filled wrap

- **pancake wrap** one buckwheat wrap (*see p.104*)

and

- **protein filling** make your own filling from foods you have available, or try recipes such as avocado and scallop (*see p.105*), smoked salmon and poached egg (*see p.59*) or wild mushroom and Parma ham (*see p.104*)

and

- **salad** if using a plain protein filling, such as cheese or grilled chicken, either add a side-salad such as the avocado and watercress salad (*see p.120*), or roll a handful of green leaves and tomato slices into the wrap

## Seared tuna with side-dish

- **seared tuna** a fresh tuna steak, seared in cinnamon or other spices (*see p.128*), or marinated in one of the marinade recipes, such as horseradish and lime or sesame oil and grainy mustard (*see p.126–27 for all recipes*)

and

- **side-dish** a portion of a vegetable-based side-dish such as ratatouille, onion and tomato niçoise, baby beets in horseradish or stir-fried vegetables (*see p.96–97 for all recipes*)

and (if lunch-time)

- **mashed potato** a tablespoon of mashed potato

## Salad plate

- **salad** choose from the recipes which contain a suitable protein serving, such as sprouted seed salad (*see p.119*), green and white salad (*see p.113*), avocado and quinoa salad (*see p.93*) or caesar salad (*see p.116*)

and (if lunch-time)

- **potatoes or couscous** a few new potatoes drizzled with walnut oil, or a small portion of couscous, brown rice or bulgar wheat

# Delicious dinners ...

Applying The Food Doctor principles to a main meal is simple: just remember the ratios (*see pp. 70–75*) and you can't go wrong.

## The usual choice

**Grilled lamb chop with roasted vegetables** This is a delicious way to eat vegetables, especially with some herbs, such as rosemary. The ratio of protein to carbohydrate is also fine, but the choice of meat could be better.

**Seared tuna with mashed potato and steamed asparagus** These foods are all healthy, nutritious and good Food Doctor choices. Mashed potato is a traditional comforting favourite and, if this meal were to be eaten at lunch-time, it would be fine. However there is a rule regarding eating starchy carbohydrates; don't do it after 7pm.

**Vegetable stir-fry with avocado and watercress salad** Stir-fries and salads are great ways of eating different varieties of vegetables with all their nutrients still intact. They are also quick options. However, there is something missing that stops this from being a healthy and complete meal.

# can be diet-friendly too

## The Food Doctor choice

Although grilling is a healthy option, a lamb chop is a relatively fatty meat cut. Red meat contains a higher amount of saturated fats than white meat.

- A grilled chicken breast has a much lower saturated fat content than lamb. Chicken is versatile and can easily be spiced up too (*see pp.130–31*).

- There is a great range of fish available and many have the added bonus of being rich in essential fats. Try red or grey mullet, sardines or swordfish, either grilled or baked.

To make this the perfect evening meal, substitute pea and ginger mash (*see p.66*) for the starchy mashed potato.

- Try some of the other delicious mashes (*see p.66–67*). They all contain some protein too, so remember that when gauging portion sizes and ensure you have enough complex carbohydrate.

- Instead of the pea mash you could try some steamed green vegetables or a vegetable side-dish (*see pp.96–97 for examples*). As long as the protein: complex carbohydrate ratio is right, feel free to experiment.

The missing element from the dinner on the left was protein. Without it you won't be receiving the slow-release glucose it contains and you may find yourself hungry again before bed-time.

- This feta, tomato and bean stir-fry (*see p.109*) is a delicious alternative. The feta, pine-nuts, and kidney beans together provide the requisite protein.

- Try a salad with a protein element, such as the avocado and quinoa (*see p.93*) or root vegetable and goat's cheese (*see p.112*).

# Lunch on the run ...

Good intentions are all very well, but what happens when you're buying lunch to go? Remember the ratios and you can easily create a healthy option.

## The usual choice

**Salad** How can you go wrong with a salad? Well, if you just eat a plain lettuce salad, you're missing out on essential food groups and not fuelling your body properly. Add some protein to complete the ratio of foods.

**Sandwich** Surely a sandwich packed with salad leaves is a healthy option? No, since it lacks a good balance of protein and complex carbohydrate. By asking for extra filling or removing one layer of bread from your sandwich, you can redress the ratio of food groups and turn your sandwich into a healthy choice.

**Vegetable soup and a roll**
This is an excellent choice for a perfect lunch on the run – if you choose the right foods in the right proportions. This choice needs additional protein and fibre to turn it into the perfect meal.

# making it healthier

## The Food Doctor choice

A salad can become a smarter choice if you know your vegetables. Eat those that are rich in vitamin C and other antioxidants, such as red peppers, raw carrots, watercress and tomatoes, and try to vary your choices to ensure you get a range of nutrients.

- Add a brown rice salad: it is high in B vitamins, so makes a good choice of lunch-time starchy complex carbohydrate.

- Protein such as chicken or tuna boosts the mineral content of your meal and makes it convert more slowly into glucose.

White bread is a poor choice as it is low in fibre and thus has a high GI value (*see p.21*). Instead, try rye bread as it is dense and allows you to vary your grain intake, or sourdough if you want to avoid yeast (in general, I believe we eat more yeast products than we should).

- Add tomato for extra fibre and antioxidants.

- Chicken, tuna, egg or smoked salmon are all good sources of protein for sandwich fillings.

- Remember to minimise mayonnaise and butter. Use seasoning instead: a layer of mustard on the bread adds flavour and a moist texture.

Favour vegetable-based soups over those based on cream or potatoes, and just add fibre and protein to make soup a smart option.

- Add some chick-peas or other pulses to boost the protein ratio of your soup, or add some tofu, shredded ham or sliced chicken breast.

- Stir in a small can of sweetcorn or some baby spinach leaves to give your soup extra fibre.

- Swap the white roll for a wholemeal or rye option to avoid high-GI refined flour products.

# Coconut chicken

**LUNCH OR DINNER**

The spices and coconut give flavour to the chicken, which can be prepared without the rice for an even quicker meal with vegetables or salad. Serves two.

**ready in 30 minutes**

1 skinless, boned chicken breast (approx. 150g/5oz)

200ml (7fl oz) coconut milk

½ teaspoon chilli paste

1–2 tablespoons chopped fresh coriander

1 garlic clove, crushed

Freshly ground black pepper

150g (5oz) brown rice

350ml (12fl oz) vegetable stock (*see p.149*)

½ teaspoon olive oil

1 small red pepper, cored, deseeded and cut into strips

Cut the chicken breast into strips. Place the coconut milk, chilli paste, coriander, garlic and black pepper in a bowl and mix well. Stir the chicken strips into the mixture. Set aside to marinate while cooking the rice.

Bring the stock to the boil in a heavy-based saucepan, add the rice, cover, and simmer for 25–30 minutes, or until the rice is cooked. Drain, stir in a little olive oil and perhaps some chopped herbs, cover and keep warm.

Heat a wok or frying pan and pour in the chicken and its marinade. Cook gently for about 5 minutes, until the chicken is almost cooked. Add the red pepper strips and cook for a further 5 minutes, until the chicken is fully cooked but the pepper is still firm. Serve at once.

## SERVING IDEAS

**For lunch** Serve exactly as the recipe suggests for a delicious lunch.

**For dinner** Omit the rice from the dish and in its place add a mixture of lightly steamed green vegetables. Or, add finely chopped vegetables such as broccolli and courgette to the stir-fry.

# Smoked fish chowder

Provided you use fresh, not frozen, fish, stock and prawns, you could make double the quantity of this recipe and freeze what you do not use. Serves two.

**ready in 30 minutes**

### SERVING IDEAS

**For lunch** Serve with a slice of rye bread.

**For dinner** Stir in a few steamed vegetables, such as broccoli florets or asparagus, or try one of the side-salads on pp.120–21.

1 tablespoon olive oil

1 leek (approx. 100g/3½oz), finely sliced

2 shallots, finely sliced

1 carrot (approx. 100g/3½oz), grated

600ml (1 pint) fish stock (*see p.149*)

2 tablespoons Thai fish sauce (optional)

1 tablespoon lemon juice

200g (7oz) smoked haddock, cod or trout, skin removed and cut into chunks

75g (2½oz) cooked prawns

Freshly ground black pepper

2–3 tablespoons live natural yoghurt

1 tablespoon chopped parsley

Heat the oil in a heavy-based saucepan, add the vegetables and cook gently until softened. Pour in the fish stock, fish sauce, if using, and lemon juice. Bring to the boil, reduce the heat and simmer for about 5 minutes.

Add the smoked fish and simmer for about 8 minutes until the fish is heated through. Add the prawns and black pepper, and simmer further until they are hot.

Put a generous tablespoon of plain yoghurt in each of two soup bowls, divide the hot chowder between the two, stir and scatter over the parsley.

# Frittatas

These frittatas are satisfying and very simple to make. You can vary the fillings according to what you have available. They can be eaten either still warm from cooking or cold with some salad. If you aren't sharing your frittata, save the other half for snacks throughout the day. Each recipe serves two.

Mediterranean frittata

## Mediterranean frittata

ready in **15** minutes

1 tablespoon olive oil

1 onion (approx. 100g/3½oz), sliced

½ red pepper, cored, deseeded and diced

½ green pepper, cored, deseeded and diced

2 medium tomatoes, sliced

4 eggs

2 tablespoons live natural yoghurt

2 tablespoons water

1 teaspoon dried mixed herbs

Freshly ground black pepper

8 black olives, pitted

Heat the oil in an omelette pan, and add the onion and diced peppers. Cook gently until softened. Add the tomatoes and cook for another 2–3 minutes.

Break the eggs into a bowl and add the yoghurt, water, herbs and black pepper to taste. Mix the ingredients together well. Pour the mixture over the vegetables in the pan, stirring gently to help the egg mixture get under the vegetables. Scatter the olives evenly over the top. Cook the frittata very gently until the bottom is firm and lightly brown. Be careful not to let it burn.

To cook the top, put the pan under a medium grill for 4–5 minutes, until it is lightly brown.

# Leek frittata

ready in **20** minutes

1 tablespoon olive oil

Juice of 1 lemon

4 medium leeks (approx 300g/10oz), finely sliced

1 tablespoon cumin seeds

4 eggs

Freshly ground black pepper

2 tablespoons live natural yoghurt

25g (¾oz) hard goat's cheese, crumbled

Heat the olive oil and lemon juice in an omelette pan, add the leeks and cook over a moderate heat for 5–10 minutes, or until soft.

While the leeks are cooking, put the cumin seeds in a small pan and toss over a high heat for a few seconds until they are just toasted.

Beat the eggs, black pepper, yoghurt and cumin seeds together, pour over the cooked leeks and cook until the underside is set and golden (about 5 minutes).

Scatter the top with grated cheese. To cook the top, put the pan under a medium grill for 4–5 minutes until it is golden.

# Sweet potato and dill frittata

ready in **25** minutes

1 small sweet potato (approx. 175g/6oz)

1 tablespoon olive oil

1 onion (approx. 125g/4oz), sliced

4 eggs

2 tablespoons live natural yoghurt

2 tablespoons water

½ teaspoon turmeric

1 teaspoon dried dill tops or 1 tablespoon chopped fresh dill

Freshly ground black pepper

Simmer the sweet potato in its skin in gently boiling water for about 15 minutes or until just soft. When cooked, peel and slice the sweet potato in half lengthways, then cut each half into slices.

Heat the oil in an omelette pan or small frying pan, add the onion and cook until softened. Break the eggs into a bowl and add the yoghurt, water, turmeric, dill and black pepper to taste. Whisk the egg mixture together well and pour over the onions in the omelette pan. Add the sweet potato and spread evenly over the contents of the pan. Cook very gently until the underside of the frittata is firm and lightly browned, being careful not to let it catch or burn.

To cook the top, put the pan under a medium grill for about 5 minutes, watching carefully, until the frittata top is brown.

# Red pesto frittata

ready in **20** minutes

4 eggs

4 tablespoons red pesto (*see p.69*)

2 tablespoons chopped fresh mint

3 tablespoons live natural yoghurt

Freshly ground black pepper

1 tablespoon olive oil

1 small onion, chopped

Break the eggs into a bowl and add the red pesto, mint, yoghurt and black pepper. Whisk everything together well.

Heat the oil in an omelette pan, add the onion and cook until softened. Pour in the egg mixture and cook over a medium heat until the frittata is firm and the base is golden. Slide the pan under a medium grill until the top of the frittata is cooked and golden.

---

**SERVING IDEAS**

**For lunch** Simply serve with a few new potatoes and some chopped tomatoes and green leaves.

**For dinner** Serve with onion and tomato nicoise or one of the other side-dishes on pp.96–97.

# Lemony spinach soup

The small dark Puy lentils give great flavour and texture to this soup. If they are not available canned, you could cook up some dried Puy lentils, or use ordinary green lentils instead. Serves two.

ready in **20** minutes

1 tablespoon olive oil

1 onion (approx. 150g/5oz), finely chopped

1 garlic clove, chopped

1 x approx. 400g (13oz) can Puy lentils, drained and rinsed

3 teaspoons bouillon powder

1 star anis

1.25 litres (2 pints) water

250g (8oz) spinach, finely shredded

3 tablespoons lemon juice

Freshly ground black pepper

2 tablespoons live natural yoghurt

Heat the olive oil in a small saucepan, add the onion and garlic and cook until softened. Set aside.

Put the lentils in a heavy-based saucepan, stir in the bouillon powder, then add the star anis and water. Bring to the boil, reduce the heat and simmer for 5–10 minutes. Add the shredded spinach and, when it has wilted, stir in the onion and garlic mixture, lemon juice and black pepper to taste.

Divide into two bowls, top each with a tablespoon of yoghurt, and serve immediately.

### SERVING IDEAS

**For lunch** Serve with a fresh wholemeal roll.

**For dinner** Everything you need is in this dish, but if you would like something extra, stir in some steamed broccoli or extra spinach.

# Seared cod on spinach

This sweet-and-sour onion sauce turns simple cod into a superbly satisfying meal. You can substitute it for any other white fish if you wish. Serves two.

**ready in 30 minutes**

2½ tablespoons olive oil, plus extra for brushing

1 onion (approx. 125g/4oz), finely sliced

1 teaspoon honey

150ml (¼ pint) fish stock (*see p.148*)

1 tablespoon white wine vinegar

1 teaspoon soy sauce

1 teaspoon mustard

Few drops Thai fish sauce (optional)

2 thick cod fillet pieces (approx. 150g/7oz each), skin on

250g (8oz) spinach

Freshly grated nutmeg

Put an oven-proof dish into a preheated oven at 200°C/400°F/gas mark 6.

To make the onion sauce, heat 2 tablespoons of the oil in a heavy-based pan over a medium heat. Cook the onion until it is soft and turning golden. Add the honey and cook for 10 minutes, or until the onion caramelises. Pour in the fish stock and vinegar and simmer for 8–10 minutes to reduce the liquid by half. Stir in the soy sauce, mustard, and Thai fish sauce, if using.

While the sauce is reducing, cook the fish. Heat the remaining olive oil in a frying pan and cook the fillets skin side down for 3–4 minutes until the skin is crisp. Brush the upper sides of the fish with a little oil.

Take the hot dish out of the oven and put the fish in it skin side up. Return the dish to the oven for 5 minutes.

Steam the spinach in a steamer set over a pan of simmering water until the leaves are just wilted. Sprinkle a little nutmeg over and keep warm until the fish is ready. Serve with the onion sauce.

**SERVING IDEAS**

**For lunch** Add a few new potatoes, drizzled over with olive oil and with sprinkled on herbs.

**For dinner** Increase the quantity of spinach or try a side-dish from pp.96–97.

# Tomatoes stuffed with quinoa

Beefsteak tomatoes are ideal for stuffing because they are large and have a firm, thick flesh that will not collapse during cooking. Here, they are stuffed with well-flavoured quinoa and given crunch with the addition of pine nuts. Serves two.

**ready in 30 minutes**

### SERVING IDEAS

**For lunch** Serve with a small baked potato and a green salad.

**For dinner** Cook up a little extra quinoa to serve on the side and eat with a side-salad or some chopped crunchy sweet peppers.

Approx. 250ml (8fl oz) vegetable stock (*see p.149*)

100g (3½oz) quinoa

2 beefsteak or other large tomatoes

Freshly ground black pepper

2 tablespoons olive oil

1 onion (approx. 100g/3½oz), chopped

1 garlic clove, chopped

1 tablespoon lemon juice

Grated zest of ½ lemon

2 tablespoons pine nuts

1 tablespoon chopped fresh coriander

2 tablespoons chopped fresh parsley

Heat the stock in a heavy-based saucepan, add the quinoa, stir and simmer for 15 minutes, or until the quinoa is tender. If the stock has not been absorbed, drain the quinoa through a sieve.

While the quinoa is cooking, slice the tops off the tomatoes and scoop out and discard the seeds, taking care not to break through the pith and skin. Grind some black pepper into the tomatoes. Preheat the oven to 180°C/350°F/gas mark 4.

Heat the oil in a heavy-based saucepan, add the onion and garlic and cook until golden. Add the quinoa, lemon juice and zest, pine nuts and chopped herbs and mix well. Spoon the mixture into the tomatoes and top with the "lids". Put the tomatoes in an oven-proof dish, cover and cook in the oven for 15 minutes, or until the tomatoes are soft.

# Thai-style chicken

This dish is very simple to create yet has a fresh exotic taste. Experiment with the herbs and spices to achieve different flavours. Serves two.

ready in **30** minutes

### SERVING IDEAS

**For lunch** Serve with brown rice. Add some chopped herbs for interest.

**For dinner** Try using extra carrots and celery to increase the meal size slightly, or add some fresh leaves as an accompaniment.

1 skinless, boned chicken breast (approx. 125g/4oz), sliced with the grain of the meat to make four equal-sized pieces

2 tablespoons lemon juice

Freshly ground black pepper

2 small leeks (approx. 150g/5oz when cleaned), finely sliced

125g (4oz) carrots, grated or cut into julienne strips

2 sticks celery, halved and finely sliced lengthways

3 spring onions, finely sliced lengthways

1 plump lemon grass stem, finely sliced

4 sprigs fresh thyme

200ml (7fl oz) vegetable stock (*see p.149*)

2 tablespoons dry white wine (optional)

Put the chicken pieces in a bowl with the lemon juice and black pepper, mix well and set aside to marinate while you prepare the vegetables.

Put the vegetables, herbs and chicken in a shallow, lidded frying pan. Add the stock, and white wine, if using. Bring to the boil, cover the pan and simmer very gently for about 20–25 minutes, until the chicken is cooked and the vegetables are tender. Serve immediately.

# Fish plaki

The tangy tomato sauce is tasty and thick, so is very filling. This dish can also be made with chicken if that is what you have available. Serves two.

ready in **30** minutes

1 tablespoon olive oil, plus extra for greasing

1 slice wholegrain or rye bread, crumbed

1 x approx. 225g (7½oz) can chopped tomatoes

2 tablespoons chopped fresh parsley

1 garlic clove, crushed

1 tablespoon lemon juice

Pinch cayenne or chilli pepper

Freshly ground black pepper

350–400g (11½–13oz) firm white fish fillets, such as cod, haddock, or orange roughy

Preheat the oven to 180°C/350°F/gas mark 4. Lightly oil an oven-proof dish.

Put the breadcrumbs, tomatoes, parsley, garlic, lemon juice and cayenne or chilli pepper in a saucepan. Add black pepper to taste, then bring to the boil and simmer for a couple of minutes, stirring well.

Put the fish in the prepared dish, brush with oil, and pour over the sauce. Cover the dish with foil and bake in the preheated oven for about 20 minutes, depending on the thickness of the fillets, until the fish is cooked through but still moist. Serve at once.

## SERVING IDEAS

**For lunch** Serve with some brown rice and ratatouille (*see p. 96*).

**For dinner** Try teaming this with one of the tasty side-dishes on pp.96–97 or one of the mashes on pp.66–67.

# Avocado and quinoa salad

This dish uses quinoa as it is a gluten-free grain that has a good protein content. Bulgar wheat or couscous would make good substitutes. Serves two.

ready in **30** minutes

250ml (8fl oz) vegetable stock (*see p.149*)

125g (4oz) quinoa

2 hen's eggs or 6 quail's eggs, hard-boiled

1 avocado

2 tablespoons lemon juice

2 spring onions, trimmed and finely sliced

100g (3½oz) small, firm mushrooms (white, brown or exotic), wiped and sliced

1 medium yellow pepper, cored, deseeded and cut into strips

6 black olives, pitted

Freshly ground black pepper

1 tablespoon chopped fresh coriander

Olive oil, to drizzle

Heat the stock in a heavy-based saucepan, pour in the quinoa and simmer for about 20 minutes, until all the stock is absorbed.

While the quinoa is cooking, peel and slice the eggs. Peel and slice the avocado (at the last minute, if possible) and sprinkle it with a little of the lemon juice so that it does not go brown.

When the quinoa is cooked, stir in the remaining lemon juice and allow the quinoa to cool a little. Then gently fold in the remaining ingredients, drizzle with olive oil and serve.

## SERVING IDEAS

**For lunch** This is already a very filling salad so can be served alone, but you could add a small jacket potato if you wish.

**For dinner** This is a substantial salad, but you could add some extra chopped salad vegetables if you wish.

# Side-dishes

These vegetable side-dishes are perfect additions to any lunch or evening meal. Each tastes just as great hot or cold, so try one as a side-dish with your dinner and save some to accompany your lunch or snack for the next day. Each recipe serves two.

## Ratatouille

| ready in 30 minutes |

Aubergines can be bitter, unless they have been salted. If you have time, slice them (reasonably finely) and layer in a colander with a sprinkling of salt between layers. Leave for at least half an hour to remove the bitter juices. Rinse, drain and pat dry.

4 tablespoons olive oil

1 aubergine (approx. 200g/7oz), trimmed and sliced moderately finely

2 courgettes (approx. 250g/8oz total weight), trimmed and sliced moderately finely

1 garlic clove, chopped

4 tomatoes (approx. 300g/10oz), roughly chopped

2 tablespoons chopped fresh parsley

Freshly ground black pepper

Heat the oil in a wide-based saucepan, add the sliced vegetables and the garlic, and cook gently for about 10 minutes, or until they are all soft and turning golden. Add the tomatoes and stir them down into the other ingredients. Stir in the parsley and black pepper to taste. Cover the pan and cook for a further 15 minutes or so over a medium heat, until all the vegetables are really soft and blend together. Stir occasionally to prevent sticking.

Note: This dish freezes well so it is a good idea to make it in bulk. You could use this ratatouille instead of the canned version needed for chick-pea and ratatouille stew (*see p.137*).

---

**SERVING IDEAS**

**For lunch** Try the onion and tomato nicoise or ratatouille stirred into pasta with some chicken or fish and save a little to eat with cubed feta as a snack.

**For dinner** Any of these side-dishes taste great with barbecued or baked chicken, or with the various salmon recipes on pp.124–25.

---

## Onion and tomato niçoise

| ready in 30 minutes |

2 tablespoons olive oil

2 onions (approx. 250g/8oz), halved lengthways and finely sliced

1 garlic clove, crushed

1 sprig fresh rosemary (or ½ teaspoon dried rosemary)

2 sprigs thyme (or 1 teaspoon dried thyme)

1 bay leaf

2–3 tomatoes (approx. 250g/8oz), sliced

12 black olives, pitted

6 anchovy fillets (washed if salted, drained if in oil), chopped

Freshly ground black pepper

Heat the oil in a large, heavy-based saucepan, add the onions, garlic, and herbs and cook gently for 20 minutes, until soft and golden. Add the tomatoes and cook for a couple of minutes until they soften, then stir in the olives and anchovy fillets. Add black pepper to taste and serve at once.

Note: If you leave the saucepan on the gentle heat for an extra hour's cooking time, the dish will be so mellowed that you will not be able tell the onions from the black olives.

## Baby beets in a horseradish sauce

ready in **15** minutes

4–6 baby beetroots (approx. 350g/11½oz)

60g (2oz) soft silken tofu (or plain tofu)

2 tablespoons horseradish sauce (*see p.149*)

2 tablespoons lemon juice

Freshly ground black pepper

Leave the tops and tails on the beetroots and make sure the skin is intact. This will prevent too much colour leeching out as the beetroots cook. Boil them in very lightly salted water for about 25 minutes, or drizzle them with a tablespoon of olive oil and roast in an oven set to 180°C/350°F/gas mark 4 for about 25 minutes.

When the beetroots are cooked, peel them, trim off the tops and tails, and cut into chunks.

To make the sauce, put the tofu, horseradish sauce, lemon juice and black pepper into a blender and blend to make a smooth sauce with a creamy consistency, adding a little water if necessary. Heat the sauce in a pan and pour over the beetroot. Serve warm as a vegetable accompaniment or cold as a salad.

## Stir-fried vegetables

ready in **10** minutes

1 tablespoon caraway seeds

1 tablespoon olive oil

150g (5oz) green cabbage (coarse centre stem removed), shredded

100g (3½oz) carrots, coarsely grated

1 tablespoon lemon juice

Heat a wok or frying pan. Put in the caraway seeds and dry-roast for 2–3 minutes. Add the olive oil and the vegetables to the pan, and stir to coat the vegetables with the oil. Add the lemon juice and stir-fry for about 5 minutes, until the vegetables are heated through.

Baby beets in a horseradish sauce

# Swordfish with coriander and lime

You could try this recipe with tuna in place of swordfish; both provide dense, meaty steaks. In the summer, try these on the barbecue. Serves two.

ready in **20** minutes

2 teaspoons coriander seeds

2 teaspoons fennel seeds

Juice of 1 lime

2 swordfish steaks (approx. 150g/5oz each)

Freshly ground black pepper

1 tablespoon olive oil

Grind the seeds together with a pestle and mortar or in a grinder, or crush them with a rolling pin. Squeeze the lime juice over the steaks and season with black pepper, then sprinkle over the ground seeds and press them in well. Set the steaks aside for about 5 minutes for the flavours to penetrate the fish.

Heat the oil in a frying pan set over a medium heat. Put in the fish steaks and cook each side for about 4 minutes. The steaks should be just cooked through and golden on the outside. Serve immediately.

## SERVING IDEAS

**For lunch** Try adding red salsa (*see p.94*) and a few cherry tomatoes with a portion of brown rice or couscous.

**For dinne**r Serve with the vegetable stir-fry or another side-dish from pp.96–97.

# Tomato and red pepper soup with cannellini beans

The beans can be swapped for other pulses depending on what you have available. The soup freezes well so try making it in bulk. Serves two.

ready in 20 minutes

1 tablespoon olive oil

1 onion (approx. 125g/4oz), finely chopped

1 garlic clove, finely chopped

1 large red pepper, cored, deseeded and chopped

1 x 400g (13oz) can chopped tomatoes

1 tablespoon tomato purée

½ teaspoon paprika

1 large sprig fresh thyme or ½ teaspoon dried thyme

1 x 400g (13oz) can cannellini beans

500ml (17fl oz) vegetable stock (*see p.149*)

Handful fresh basil leaves, shredded, to garnish

Heat the olive oil in a heavy-based saucepan, add the onion, garlic and red pepper and cook until softened but not coloured.

Add the remaining ingredients. Bring the mixture to the boil, reduce the heat and simmer gently for 15 minutes. Scatter over the basil leaves before serving.

## SERVING IDEAS

**For lunch** Serve with a slice of wholemeal or rye bread.

**For dinner** Introduce some extra chopped vegetables to the soup, such as fennel, celery, broccoli or cabbage, at the same stage as you add the peppers.

# Healthy soups

These soups are a great option for a quick dinner or lunch. They can all be kept chilled in the fridge for up to three days, so they are good options for making in bulk to save time on preparation. The gazpacho and mushroom soups can also be frozen for up to a month. All are complete meals that include protein, and all serve two.

---

### SERVING IDEAS

**For lunch** Serve with a piece of rye bread or a crusty wholemeal roll.

**For dinner** Add a few extra vegetables to the soup to increase the complex carbohydrate ratio.

---

Prawn and watercress soup

# Prawn and watercress soup

ready in **10** minutes

2 bunches watercress (approx. 150g/5oz), roughly shredded

Approx. 45g (1½oz) baby spinach leaves, coarsely chopped

3 large stalks parsley

2 sprigs mint

600ml (1 pint) vegetable stock (*see p.149*)

Juice of ½ lemon

Freshly ground black pepper

6 tablespoons live natural yoghurt

1 egg

12–16 cooked prawns

Mint or basil, to garnish

Put all the ingredients, except the prawns and garnish, in a blender. Blend thoroughly to make a very fine mixture. Pour into a saucepan and heat gently until simmering. Although the egg prevents the yoghurt curdling, the soup should still not be boiled hard or simmered for too long.

Divide the prawns between two bowls, pour on the soup and serve garnished with the mint or basil.

# Mushroom and lentil soup

ready in **30** minutes

300g (10oz) mushrooms, roughly chopped

150g (5oz) onion, chopped

2 tablespoons olive oil

1 bay leaf

3 sprigs fresh thyme or 1 teaspoon dried thyme

600ml (1 pint) vegetable stock (*see p.149*)

2 tablespoons tomato purée

Freshly ground black pepper

1 tablespoon mushroom ketchup (or soy sauce, if preferred)

1 x approx. 400g (13oz) can lentils, drained and rinsed

2 tablespoons live natural yoghurt

Put the mushrooms and onion in a food processor and blend until the vegetables form a paste.

Heat the oil in a heavy-based saucepan, add the mushroom and onion paste and the herbs. Cook for 5 minutes. Add the stock, tomato purée, black pepper and ketchup or soy sauce, bring to the boil, then simmer for 20 minutes.

Remove the whole herbs from the pan, then stir in the lentils. Heat through for about 5 minutes. Divide the soup between two bowls, stir a tablespoon of yoghurt into each and serve immediately.

# Very quick gazpacho

ready in **10** minutes

1 x approx. 400g (13oz) can tomatoes

1 red onion (approx. 150g/5oz), roughly chopped

1 pepper, any colour, cored, deseeded and roughly chopped

½ cucumber (approx. 150g/5oz), roughly chopped

1 tablespoon lemon juice

1 tablespoon olive oil

1 tablespoon tomato purée

300ml (½ pint) mixed vegetable juice

Large sprig parsley

2–3 sprigs basil

Freshly ground black pepper

90g (3oz) flaked cooked fish, chicken, or smoked mackerel, or 4 tablespoons chick-peas

Finely chopped spring onion, cucumber and tomato, mixed, to garnish

Put all the ingredients into a blender (including the juice from the can of tomatoes), except the fish or chicken and the garnish mixture. Blend until smooth.

Divide the fish or chicken between two bowls and pour over the cold soup. Top with a tablespoon of the garnish mixture before serving.

# Chicken and cashew stir-fry

Stir-fries are a healthy option because they use little oil and the vegetables can be just lightly cooked and so retain their nutrients. Serves two.

**ready in 20 minutes**

**SERVING IDEAS**

**For lunch** Serve with buckwheat noodles.

**For dinner** At the same time as you add the broccoli, mix in a few extra vegetables, such as mushrooms, mange-tout or pak choi, to boost the complex carbohydrate content of this dish.

1 skinless, boned chicken breast (approx. 150g/5oz)

1 teaspoon five-spice paste (*see p.148*)

1 teaspoon tamarind paste (*see p.149*)

1 tablespoon soy sauce

1 garlic clove

Juice of ½ lemon

1 tablespoon white wine or water

60g (2oz) unsalted cashew nuts

1 tablespoon olive oil

125g (4oz) broccoli, broken into small florets

2 spring onions, trimmed and cut lengthways into 7cm (3in) strips

Cut the chicken into strips. Place the five-spice and tamarind pastes, soy sauce, garlic, lemon juice and wine or water in a bowl and mix well together. Add the chicken strips and set aside to marinate for as much time as you have (about 30 minutes is preferable).

Heat a wok or frying pan, add the cashew nuts and dry-roast, turning often, until golden. Tip out of the pan and set aside.

Pour the olive oil into the pan and heat gently. Lift the chicken strips from the marinade with a slotted spoon, add to the pan and stir-fry for about 5 minutes. Add the marinade, broccoli and spring onions to the pan and continue cooking for another 5 minutes, adding a little more water if the contents begin to look a little dry. Finally, stir in the cashew nuts, and serve.

# Vegetable and bean soup

This recipe makes approximately eight servings. Any left over can be kept in the fridge for up to three days or frozen for up to one month.

**ready in** 25 **minutes**

2 tablespoons olive oil

2 onions (approx. 300g/10oz), chopped

2 garlic cloves, chopped

2 celery stalks, trimmed and finely sliced

100g (3½oz) round green beans, trimmed and cut into 3cm (1¼in) pieces

1 teaspoon freshly ground coriander seeds

1 x approx. 400g (13oz) can chopped tomatoes

1 litre (1¾ pints) vegetable stock *(see p.149)*

100g (3½oz) green cabbage, shredded

2 carrots (approx. 200g/7oz), grated

1 x approx. 400g (13oz) can cannellini beans

Grated hard goat's cheese or other hard cheese, to garnish

Heat the oil in a large, heavy-based saucepan and add the onions. Cook gently over a medium heat for about 5 minutes, until the onions are softened.

Add the garlic, celery, green beans and ground coriander to the pan, stir well and cook for 5 minutes. Add the tomatoes and stock and simmer for a further 5 minutes. Add the cabbage, carrots and cannellini beans and simmer together for 5–10 minutes.

Serve with a little grated cheese sprinkled over.

## SERVING IDEAS

**For lunch** This soup already contains everything you need for a warming lunch. Serve with a wholemeal roll.

**For dinner** Add some extra celery, green beans and cabbage if you wish, or serve with green leaves or other side-salad *(see pp.120–21)*.

# Wraps and fillings

If you make a batch of the basic pancake wrap recipe, store the wraps in the fridge for one day, or freeze them for up to one month. When freezing, separate them with cling film. To reheat them, add one at a time to a small frying pan. When the first side is hot, flip it over. The basic recipes makes eight pancakes and each recipe filling serves two.

## Basic pancake wraps

ready in **20** minutes

100g (3½oz) buckwheat flour

1 large egg

300ml (½ pint) liquid, use 150ml/¼ pint each milk and water, or all water

Freshly ground black pepper

Put the flour into a large bowl. Make a well in the middle and break in the egg. Using a whisk, gradually add the liquid, whisking well, until the mixture has the consistency of thin cream. Depending on the size of the egg, you may need a little more or less fluid than the quantity specified. Grind over some black pepper.

Heat a flat-based frying pan or griddle until hot, wiping a little light-flavoured oil over it with kitchen paper while it is still quite cool. When hot, pour an eighth of the mixture into the centre of the pan, tilting the pan to spread the mixture. Cook for a minute or two, until the pancake begins to bubble round the edge. Flip it over with a spatula and continue cooking for another minute or two.

When the pancake is cooked, turn it on to a plate lined with cling film and continue making pancakes – the mixture should make eight pancakes. As you make them, continue to stack the pancakes, separated by cling film, on the plate.

## Wild mushroom and Parma ham wrap

ready in **15** minutes

2 tablespoons olive oil

250g (8oz) mixed wild mushrooms, sliced

6 sun-dried tomatoes in olive oil, cut in strips

Zest of ½ lemon

1 tablespoon chopped fresh parsley

Freshly ground black pepper

2 pancake wraps (*see left*)

2 handfuls mixed salad leaves

Walnut oil, to drizzle

2 slices Parma ham, cut into strips

1 tablespoon lemon juice

Heat the olive oil in a frying pan, add the mushrooms, tomatoes and lemon zest and cook for about 10 minutes, or until the mushrooms are cooked. Stir in the parsley and black pepper.

Place each wrap on a plate, put a handful of salad leaves on each and drizzle over the walnut oil. Put half the mushroom mixture, a slice of Parma ham and some lemon juice on each and roll them up to finish.

Wild mushroom and Parma ham wrap

## Sesame, spinach and poached egg wrap

ready in **10** minutes

1 heaped tablespoon sesame seeds

2 tablespoons olive oil

1 small onion, finely chopped

1 garlic clove, chopped

250g (8oz) fresh spinach, washed and coarsely shredded

1 tablespoon lemon juice

Freshly ground black pepper

2 eggs

2 pancake wraps (*see opposite*)

Heat a wok or frying pan, put in the sesame seeds and dry-roast gently until golden. Set the sesame seeds aside in a small bowl.

Heat the olive oil in the pan, add the onion and garlic and cook until they are turning golden. Add the spinach leaves, lemon juice and pepper. Stir-fry until the spinach is wilted then set aside.

Break the eggs into a saucer and slide them into a pan of boiling water to which a dash of vinegar has been added. Poach the eggs until firm, then lift them from the pan with a slotted spoon and set aside to drain while you reheat or make the pancakes.

Put half the spinach mixture and one egg on a pancake, sprinkle over half the sesame seeds, and fold the pancake over. Leave in the pan for a few minutes for everything to heat together. Repeat with the second pancake.

## Asian-style squid wrap

ready in **20** minutes

250g (8oz) squid (cleaned weight), cleaned and cartilage removed

6cm (2½in) piece from the fat end of a lemon grass stalk, finely sliced

1½ tablespoons lime juice

1 tablespoon Thai fish sauce

1cm (½ inch) piece fresh root ginger, peeled and grated

2 spring onions, trimmed and sliced

½ orange, yellow or red pepper, cored, deseeded and chopped

2 pancake wraps (*see opposite*)

Large handful of mixed salad leaves

Walnut or sesame oil, to drizzle

Few basil leaves

Few coriander leaves

Slice the squid sacs into rings and roughly chop the tentacles. Drop them into a pan of boiling water and simmer for about one minute, or until the pieces are opaque and tender. Drain and set aside.

Place the lemongrass in a bowl with the lime juice, fish sauce, ginger, spring onions and pepper. Add the squid and mix everything well.

Place each wrap on a plate and divide the salad leaves between them. Drizzle some oil over the leaves and top each wrap with half the squid mixture. Tear a few basil and coriander leaves over each and roll them up.

Note: If you wish, the squid may be replaced by tuna or cooked prawns.

## Avocado and scallop wrap

ready in **10** minutes

1 ripe avocado, peeled and cubed

8 ripe cherry tomatoes, quartered

1 tablespoon snipped chives

2 handfuls mixed salad leaves

1 tablespoon olive oil

4 scallops with corals and whites separated, whites halved

2 pancake wraps (*see opposite*)

**For the dressing:**

3 tablespoons olive oil

1 tablespoon lime juice

1 tablespoon chopped parsley

1 teaspoon Dijon mustard

Freshly ground black pepper

To make the dressing, place all the ingredients in a bowl and mix well.

Put the avocado, tomatoes and chives in a bowl and cover with two-thirds of the dressing. Set aside. Gently heat the olive oil in a frying pan, cook the scallop pieces for 2 minutes on each side.

Place each wrap on a plate. Divide the salad leaves, avocado mixture and remaining dressing between them and top with the scallops, then roll them up.

# Leeks in red pesto and tofu sauce

A delicious way of cooking leeks, this recipe works just as well with bulbs of fennel, which should be quartered or cut into thick slices before steaming. Serves two.

**ready in 20 minutes**

### SERVING IDEAS

**For lunch** Serve with some rye bread and mixed leaves drizzled with a dressing *(see pp.114–15)*.

**For dinner** Add an extra leek to the recipe or try a mixture of both fennel and leek.

4 medium leeks

4 tablespoons red pesto (*see p.69*)

75g (2½oz) tofu

Juice of ½ lemon

125–150ml (4–5fl oz) vegetable stock (*see p.149*)

Freshly ground black pepper

30g (1oz) hard goat's cheese or other hard cheese, finely grated

Trim and wash the leeks and slice each one in half vertically. Place in a steamer or in a lidded colander over a saucepan of boiling water and steam for about 10–15 minutes, until soft.

Meanwhile, mix the red pesto, tofu and lemon juice together in a bowl and add sufficient stock or vegetable juice to make a thick pouring sauce. Pour into a saucepan and bring to simmering point. Add black pepper to taste.

When the leeks are cooked, put them in a heat-proof dish, pour over the sauce, and scatter the grated cheese on top. Place under a hot grill for a couple of minutes until the cheese has browned on top, then serve.

# Cajun-style fish fry

The sweetcorn cobs could be replaced with kernels, if you prefer. If you don't have any onion powder, use some finely chopped onion instead. Serves two.

ready in 15 minutes

250g (8oz) firm white fish fillets, such as cod, haddock or orange roughy, cut into chunks

½ teaspoon each paprika, cinnamon, nutmeg, ginger, black pepper, and onion powder, mixed

60g (2oz) baby sweetcorn cobs, thickly sliced, or 60g (2oz) sweetcorn kernels

125g (4oz) sugar snap peas, trimmed

1 courgette (approx. 125g/4oz), thickly sliced

2 tablespoons olive oil

Juice of ½ lemon

Chopped fresh coriander, to garnish

### SERVING IDEAS

**For lunch** Serve with buckwheat noodles or brown rice and a mixed leaf salad.

**For dinner** Add some extra fibrous vegetables to the stir-fry, such as broccoli or cabbage.

Put the fish in a bowl, sprinkle over the mixed spices and toss together well. Set aside to marinate.

Place the vegetables in a small pan, pour in water to just cover them and bring to the boil. Simmer for about half a minute, then drain the vegetables.

Heat the olive oil to hot in a wok or frying pan, add the fish chunks and stir-fry carefully for about 5 minutes, until cooked through and golden brown. Do not let the fish chunks fall to pieces. Lift them from the pan with a slotted spoon and set aside.

Add the vegetables and lemon juice to the pan and stir-fry for 5 minutes or so, until the vegetables are hot. Carefully stir in the fish and scatter the coriander over the top, then serve.

# Seared tuna with beans and pasta

If you don't have any fresh tuna available, make this dish with canned tuna, choosing a variety canned in spring water rather than oil or brine. Serves two.

ready in **20** minutes

90g (3oz) pasta (use buckwheat, corn or wholemeal)
2 teaspoons olive oil
100g (3½oz) green beans, trimmed and cut in half
½ red or orange pepper, cored, deseeded and sliced
1 x 150g (5oz) fresh tuna steak
30g (1oz) red onion, very finely sliced

**For the dressing:**
4 tablespoons olive oil
2 tablespoons lemon juice
1 garlic clove, crushed
2 tablespoons chopped fresh parsley

Cook the pasta according to the instructions on the packet. Drain through a colander and return to the empty pan. Drizzle over a teaspoonful of the olive oil to prevent sticking and set aside.

Steam the beans and pepper over a pan of gently simmering water for about 5 minutes, or until cooked but still firm.

If using fresh tuna, brush with olive oil and sear in a pan or under a hot grill, turning at least once, for 6–8 minutes, or until just cooked. Break into chunks.

To make the dressing, put all the ingredients in a bowl and mix well with a fork.

Put the pasta, beans, pepper, tuna chunks and red onion in a large serving bowl. (If you are using canned tuna, add it at this point also.) Pour over the dressing, and toss to mix everything together well. Serve at once.

# Smoked chicken in sweet chilli sauce

LUNCH OR DINNER

If you do not have smoked chicken, use cooked chicken instead – perhaps left-overs from a grilled or roasted chicken. Serves two.

**ready in 10 minutes**

### SERVING IDEAS

**For lunch** Serve with some brown rice or buckwheat noodles.

**For dinner** Add a handful of spinach, broccoli florets or any other green vegetables at the same time as the mangetout.

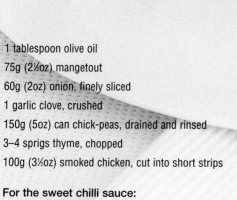

1 tablespoon olive oil

75g (2½oz) mangetout

60g (2oz) onion, finely sliced

1 garlic clove, crushed

150g (5oz) can chick-peas, drained and rinsed

3–4 sprigs thyme, chopped

100g (3½oz) smoked chicken, cut into short strips

**For the sweet chilli sauce:**

1 heaped teaspoon chilli paste

2 tablespoons orange juice

1 teaspoon lemon juice

1 scant teaspoon honey, made up to 60ml (2fl oz) with 3 tablespoons water

First, make the sweet chilli sauce. Put all the ingredients in a bowl and whisk together with a fork.

Heat the oil in a wok or frying pan, add the mangetout and onion and cook until the onion is soft. Add the garlic, chick-peas and sweet chilli sauce, and cook until the chick-peas are hot. Add the thyme and chicken and continue to cook, stirring, until the chicken is hot, then serve.

# Root vegetable and goat's cheese salad

**LUNCH OR DINNER**

For this substantial salad use celeriac and carrot as the base vegetables and then add your favourite root vegetables. Experiment with sweet potatoes, swedes or parsnips. Serves two.

**ready in 10 minutes**

## SERVING IDEAS

**For lunch** Serve with a chunk of soda bread or a spoonful of couscous.

**For dinner** Increase the quantity of root vegetables and add another five cubes or so of goat's cheese.

200g (7oz) root vegetables, coarsely grated

2 tablespoons olive oil

1 tablespoon black mustard seeds

30g (1oz) walnut pieces

25g (¾oz) raisins

100g (3½oz) hard goat's cheese, such as goat's cheddar, cubed

sesame oil, to drizzle

1–2 tablespoons chopped fresh coriander

Place the grated vegetables in a large bowl. Heat the oil in a small pan and when hot add the black mustard seeds. When the seeds start to pop, pour them over the vegetables. Stir in the walnuts, raisins and goat's cheese. Drizzle with sesame oil and sprinkle over the coriander.

# Green and white salad

As all the ingredients in this salad are quite delicately flavoured, you could choose a tangy dressing to dress it. Serves two.

**ready in 10 minutes**

100g (3½oz) cauliflower, broken into small florets

100g (3½oz) broccoli, broken into small florets

1 small carrot, grated

75g (2½oz) feta or smoked tofu, cut into chunks

2 tablespoons pumpkin seeds

2–3 tablespoons dressing (*choose from the dressings on pp.114–15*)

Put all the ingredients except the dressing in a salad bowl. Sprinkle over the dressing and toss everything together so that the vegetables are well coated in the dressing, then serve.

**SERVING IDEAS**

**For lunch** Serve with a few new potatoes drizzled with olive oil.

**For dinner** Add a few extra broccoli or cauliflower florets.

# Asian fish cakes

These are so delicious you may not have left-overs, but, if you do, mash them with a little salsa to make a great snack topping for oatcakes. Serves two.

ready in **20** minutes

200g (7oz) white fish fillets, cut into chunks

4 spring onions, trimmed and chopped

1 teaspoon grated fresh root ginger

1 teaspoon green curry paste

2 teaspoons Thai fish sauce

1 egg

2 tablespoons chopped coriander or parsley

2 tablespoons flour (gluten-free flour, rice flour or cornflour)

Zest of 1 lime

1 tablespoon lime juice

Freshly ground black pepper

## SERVING IDEAS

**For lunch** Serve the fish cakes with red or green salsa (*see pp.94–95*), new potatoes and steamed vegetables or a green salad.

**For dinner** Try the cakes with the fennel and carrot side salad, or another from pp.120–21.

Place the fish chunks, spring onions, ginger, curry paste, fish sauce, egg and herbs in a food processor and blend until the mixture is fairly smooth, but still has some texture.

Scrape the mixture into a bowl. Add the flour, lime zest and juice and black pepper and stir gently to mix it all together. Divide the mixture into eight portions and, with lightly-floured hands, form each portion into a ball.

The fish cakes may be steamed or shallow-fried. To steam them, place them in a steamer over simmering water and steam for 10 minutes. To fry them, slightly flatten each ball. Heat 3–4 tablespoons of olive oil in a shallow frying pan, add the fish cakes and cook them gently for 5–8 minutes, turning them at intervals, until they are golden brown and cooked through.

Serve 4 fish cakes per portion.

# Sprouted seed salad

There is an enormous choice of sprouts available in health-food stores and also in some supermarkets. They are incredibly nutritious and are packed with amino acids and antioxidant vitamins and minerals. You could even grow your own sprouted seeds in only a few days. Serves two.

ready in **10** minutes

250g (8oz) mixed sprouted seeds and beans

1 large crisp eating apple, cored and sliced

1 yellow pepper, cored, deseeded and cut into strips

4 tablespoons chopped mixed fresh herbs (choose from parsley, coriander, chives, dill, fennel, oregano, mint and basil)

100ml (3½fl oz) dressing (*see pp.114–15*)

Put all the ingredients into a large salad bowl and toss gently to mix everything together well.

## SERVING IDEAS

**For lunch** Add a small jacket potato or a portion of brown rice.

**For dinner** Mix in a few yellow pepper strips, or other salad vegetables you may have available.

# Side-salads

These fresh and nutritious salads are simple to make. Try them with the dressings on pp.114–15, then serve with the protein of your choice. They deliver a powerful punch of antioxidants, folate and potassium for a healthy immune system. Each recipe serves two.

## Avocado and watercress salad

ready in **5** minutes

60g (2oz) watercress, coarsely torn

Small handful rocket, coarsely torn

12 baby tomatoes, halved

1 avocado, peeled, stoned and cut into chunks

4 closed-cup white mushrooms, sliced

2–3 tablespoons dressing of your choice (*see pp.114–15*)

Mix the watercress and rocket in the bottom of a salad bowl, and pile the tomatoes, avocado and mushrooms into the middle.

Drizzle the dressing over the top, being sure to cover the avocado chunks well to preserve their pretty green colour. If you would prefer, use just a drizzle of walnut or olive oil instead of the dressing.

## Red and white cabbage salad

ready in **10** minutes

2 heaped teaspoons caraway seeds

125g (4oz) white cabbage, grated

75g (2½oz) red cabbage, grated

2–3 tablespoons dressing of your choice (*see pp.114–15*)

Put the caraway seeds in a heavy-based pan and dry-roast them over a moderate heat for about 5 minutes, tossing occasionally.

Combine both grated cabbages in a bowl and drizzle over the dressing. Mix together gently – and watch the red cabbage make pink trails through the salad. Top with the roasted caraway seeds and serve.

## Fennel and carrot salad

ready in **10** minutes

1 bulb fennel (approx. 125g/4oz), trimmed and feathery fronds reserved

2 carrots (approx. 125g/4oz), coarsely grated

Juice of 1 lemon

2 teaspoons olive oil

2 teaspoons poppy seeds

Cut the fennel bulb in half lengthways and finely slice across each half. Put the slices in a salad bowl and add the grated carrot and lemon juice.

Heat the olive oil in a small heavy-based pan over a moderate heat, then add the poppy seeds. Once the seeds start to pop, pour them and the oil over the salad and toss it well. Serve garnished with a few of the reserved fennel fronds.

# High C salad

| ready in | 5 | minutes |

2 medium tomatoes, sliced

½ cucumber, halved lengthways and sliced

1 kiwifruit, peeled, halved lengthways and sliced

2 tablespoons olive oil

2 tablespoons lemon juice

Freshly ground black pepper

Fresh basil, to garnish

Place all the ingredients, except the basil, in a salad bowl. Use a fork and spoon to toss the ingredients gently, but thoroughly, together. Garnish with shredded basil leaves.

High C salad

## SERVING IDEAS

**For lunch** Try any of these salads with some grilled fish or chicken and a small jacket potato.

**For dinner** Don't have potatoes with these salads at dinner-time. Instead try any of them with a spicy chicken recipe from pp.130–31.

# Coconut and coriander fish with couscous

LUNCH OR DINNER

Orange roughy is light and delicately flavoured, but cod or monkfish fillets could easily be used instead, if that is what you have available. Serves two.

ready in **15** minutes

### SERVING IDEAS

**For lunch** Serve with chopped cherry tomatoes and cucumber added to the couscous.

**For dinner** Omit the couscous and in its place serve one of the side-salads from pp.120–21.

2 fillets (approx. 300g/10oz total weight) orange roughy

Juice of 1 lime

Freshly ground black pepper

1 tablespoon olive oil

1 heaped teaspoon mustard seeds

2 small dried red chillies

1 garlic clove, finely chopped

1 small onion, finely sliced

2 tomatoes, sliced

60g (2oz) block creamed coconut, or 75ml (4fl oz) coconut milk

1 teaspoon coriander seeds, crushed

2 tablespoons water

1 tablespoon chopped fresh coriander

**For the couscous:**

125g (4oz) couscous

175ml (6fl oz) lightly salted boiling water

2 teaspoons olive oil

1 tablespoon each chopped fresh parsley and coriander

Preheat the oven to 140°C/275°F/gas mark 1. Cut each fillet into 3 pieces. Sprinkle with half the lime juice and some black pepper and set aside.

Put the couscous in an oven-proof bowl with the boiling water. Stir with a fork until the water is absorbed. Stir in the olive oil. Cover with foil and keep warm in the oven.

Heat the olive oil to medium-high in a wok or frying pan, add the mustard seeds and chillies and cook for 2 minutes. Add the garlic and onion and cook until the onion begins to colour.

Mix in the tomatoes, coconut, crushed coriander seeds, remaining lime juice and water. Stir-fry for 1–2 minutes. Add the fish and any juice and spoon the sauce over it. Cook very gently for about 5–6 minutes, until the fish is opaque.

Remove the coucous from the oven, stir in the herbs, and serve with the fish scattered with coriander.

# Chicken in summer herbs with mixed-bean salad

**LUNCH OR DINNER**

This mixed-bean salad makes a substantial side dish, perfect for either lunch or dinner. Substitute thyme for rosemary for a different twist. Serves two.

**ready in 20 minutes**

1 tablespoon olive oil

250–300g (8–10oz) chicken breast, cut into thick strips

1 garlic clove, chopped

8 spring onions, trimmed

2 generous tablespoons chopped mixed fresh herbs (such as parsley, thyme, sage, chives, marjoram, basil and tarragon)

2 tablespoons lemon juice

Freshly ground black pepper

**For the mixed-bean salad:**

1 x approx. 250g (8oz) can mixed beans, drained and rinsed

4 sprigs fresh thyme (or 1 teaspoon dried)

100ml (3½fl oz) hot vegetable stock (*see p.149*)

1 tablespoon chopped fresh parsley

1 tablespoon olive oil

Juice of ½ lemon

Heat the oil in a frying pan with a lid, add the chicken strips and brown them lightly on all sides, turning them frequently to prevent them sticking to the pan. Reduce the heat, toss in the spring onions, mixed herbs, lemon juice and black pepper and cover the pan. Cook gently for about 10 minutes, stirring occasionally, until the chicken is cooked through but still moist.

Make the bean salad while the chicken is cooking. First, put the beans in a saucepan with the stock and thyme. Simmer uncovered until the stock is absorbed, around 5 minutes. Pick out the fresh thyme and serve with the parsley, olive oil and lemon juice mixed in.

**SERVING IDEAS**

**For lunch** Add some rice or chopped new potatoes to the salad.

**For dinner** Serve the dish as it is but add a small side-salad of mixed green leaves. For a lighter option, substitute the mixed-bean salad with ratatouille (*see p.96*).

# Simple salmon

Salmon fillets have firm flesh with a fine texture and are free of bones. They work well with a great variety of flavourful ingredients, as in these four recipes, which can be served hot or cold. Marinate the salmon fillets in their parcels for about 15–20 minutes, so that the flavours of the ingredients are well absorbed. If you have time, experiment, too, with any other fish, such as cod, tuna or monkfish, that you have available. Each recipe serves two.

---

**SERVING IDEAS**

**For lunch** Any of these recipes would work well with some steamed vegetables and new potatoes.

**For dinner** A peppery green salad of rocket and watercress makes an ideal simple accompaniment.

---

Lime and dill
salmon fillets

## Lime and dill salmon

2 salmon fillets (approx. 150g/5oz each), skin on

2 tablespoons lime juice

2 teaspoons grated fresh root ginger

½ teaspoon anchovy essence (or 1 anchovy fillet in oil, drained and crushed)

6 large sprigs fresh dill

Freshly ground black pepper

Scrape any loose scales off the salmon fillets' skin and place each fillet, skin side down, on a square of foil large enough to fold over as a parcel.

Put the lime juice, ginger and anchovy essence or anchovy fillet, in a bowl, mix well and pour half the mixture over each salmon fillet. Top each with 2 sprigs of dill and a few twists of black pepper. Fold the foil loosely into parcels and set aside for the fish to absorb the flavours while you prepare the rest of the meal.

A few minutes before you wish to cook the fish, preheat the oven to 150°C/300°F/gas mark 2. Cook the fish for 10–15 minutes until it is cooked through but still moist. Serve sprinkled with the juices from the parcels and garnished with the remaining dill.

## Coconut and coriander salmon

ready in 20 minutes

2 salmon fillets (approx. 150g/5oz each), skin on

Approx. 15g (½oz) creamed coconut, finely grated, or 1½ tablespoons coconut milk

2 tablespoons lemon juice

Freshly ground black pepper

6 large sprigs fresh coriander

Scrape any loose scales off the salmon fillets' skin and place each fillet, skin side down, on a square of foil large enough to fold over into a parcel.

Sprinkle half the coconut and lemon juice over each fillet and season them with black pepper. Top the fillets with 2 sprigs of coriander. Fold the foil loosely into parcels and set aside for the fish to absorb the other flavours while you prepare the rest of the meal.

A few minutes before you are ready to cook the fish, preheat the oven to 150°C/300°F/gas mark 2. Bake the fish for 10–15 minutes, until it is cooked through but still moist. Serve sprinkled with the juices from the parcels and garnished with the remaining coriander.

## Fennel and grapefruit salmon

ready in 20 minutes

2 salmon fillets (approx. 150g/5oz each), skin on

2 tablespoons grapefruit juice

½ teaspoon anchovy essence (or 1 anchovy fillet in oil, drained and crushed)

6 sprigs fresh fennel

Freshly ground black pepper

Scrape any scales off the salmon fillets' skin and place each fillet, skin side down, on a square of foil large enough to fold over into a parcel.

Place the grapefruit juice and anchovy essence or anchovy fillet in a bowl, whisk together with a fork and spoon half the mixture over each fillet. Top with two sprigs of fennel and a good grind of black pepper. Fold the foil loosely into parcels and leave to stand while you prepare the rest of the meal.

A few minutes before you are ready to cook the fish, preheat the oven to 150°C/300°F/gas mark 2. Cook the fish for 10–15 minutes, until it is cooked through but still moist. Serve sprinkled with the juices from the parcels and garnished with the remaining fennel sprigs.

## Soy and spring onion salmon

ready in 20 minutes

2 salmon fillets (approx. 150g/5oz each), skin on

2 tablespoons orange juice

1 tablespoon soy sauce

2 spring onions, trimmed and very finely sliced

6 sprigs fresh thyme

Scrape any loose scales off the salmon fillets' skin and place each fillet, skin side down, on a square of foil large enough to fold over into a parcel.

Put the orange juice and soy sauce in a small bowl and whisk together. Scatter the spring onion slices evenly over the two fillets. Pour over the juice mixture and top each fillet with 2 thyme sprigs. Fold the foil loosely into a parcel and leave to stand while you prepare the rest of the meal.

A few minutes before you wish to cook the fish, preheat the oven to 150°C/300°F/gas mark 2. Cook the fish for 10–15 minutes until it is cooked through but still moist. Serve sprinkled with the juices from the parcels and garnished with the remaining thyme.

# Quick marinades

Marinades add flavour to meat and fish and help tenderise the portions before they are quickly seared on a barbecue, grill pan or under a grill. Marinate the food as long as you can, so that it really absorbs the flavours of the marinade ingredients. Just 15–20 minutes marinating while the rest of a meal is prepared works wonders with many cuts of meat and fish or even tofu.

## Chilli, lime and garlic marinade

ready in **5** minutes

1 tablespoon olive oil

2 garlic cloves, crushed

½ teaspoon chilli paste

¼ teaspoon cayenne pepper

1 teaspoon paprika

Zest and juice of 1 lime

Combine all the ingredients in a bowl, add the chosen chicken or fish and stir or rub well to cover.

The marinade will keep for 3–4 days in a screw-top jar in the fridge.

## Horseradish and lime marinade

ready in **5** minutes

1 tablespoon horseradish sauce (*see p.149*)

1 tablespoon lime juice

½–1 tablespoon live natural yoghurt

1 tablespoon olive oil

Freshly ground black pepper

Put all the ingredients in a bowl and mix them well together. Pour over fish or meat.

The marinade will keep for 2–3 days in a screw-top jar in the fridge.

## Sesame oil and grainy mustard marinade

ready in **5** minutes

1 tablespoon wholegrain mustard

2 tablespoons sesame oil

1 tablespoon lemon juice

1 tablespoon orange juice

Freshly ground black pepper

Put all the ingredients in a bowl and mix well together. Rub in to the fish or meat.

The marinade will keep for 3–4 days in a screw-top jar in the fridge.

Sesame oil and grainy mustard

Chilli, lime and garlic marinade

Horseradish and lime marinade

# Tamarind and five-spice marinade

ready in **5** minutes

2 spring onions, trimmed and cut into 2 or 3 pieces

2 tablespoons soy sauce

1 heaped teaspoon tamarind paste (*see p. 149*)

Scant teaspoon honey

1 garlic clove, crushed

1 tablespoon five-spice paste (*see p.148*)

1 tablespoon cider vinegar

100ml (3½fl oz) water

Put all the ingredients in a heavy-based saucepan, bring to the boil and boil steadily for 2 minutes.

The marinade may be used immediately, or cooled, poured into a screw-top jar and stored in the fridge for 2–3 days.

# Yoghurt and ginger marinade

ready in **5** minutes

3 tablespoons live natural yoghurt

1 rounded teaspoon grated fresh root ginger

½ teaspoon turmeric

1 garlic clove, chopped

Freshly ground black pepper

Put all the ingredients in a bowl and mix them well together. Not only does the turmeric have a lovely subtle flavour, it also adds a wonderful colour to the meat or fish marinated in the mixture.

The marinade will keep for 2–3 days in a screw-top jar in the fridge.

## SERVING IDEAS

**For lunch** Choose your favourite marinade, add it to your choice of protein and serve it with some new potatoes and a green salad.

**For dinner** The heat of the chilli, lime and garlic marinade goes deliciously well on fish, chicken or tofu alongside the fresh and tangy high C salad (*see p.121*).

Yoghurt and ginger marinade

Tamarind and five-spice marinade

# Cinnamon-seared tuna

LUNCH OR DINNER

Tuna is a fantastic protein option. It is a versatile, lean and succulent fish that in this dish looks stunning enough for a dinner party. Serves two.

**ready in 20 minutes**

1 heaped teaspoon ground cinnamon

1 teaspoon ground ginger

1 teaspoon chilli powder

2 tuna steaks (approx. 150g/5oz each)

2 tablespoons olive oil

Put the cinnamon, ginger and chilli powder in a small bowl and stir well to mix. Rub each steak well on both sides first with the olive oil and then with the spice mixture. Set aside for 10–15 minutes so that the tuna absorbs the flavour of the spice mixture.

Heat a griddle pan. When it is hot, put the tuna steaks in and sear for 3–4 minutes each side. Alternatively, place under a hot grill and sear the tuna steaks, again for 3–4 minutes each side. Do not overcook the fish, it should be only just cooked and still juicy when you serve it.

## SERVING IDEAS

**For lunch** Spiced rice (*see p.133*) will go very well with this tuna.

**For dinner** Serve with a large portion of the pea, ginger and tapenade mash (*see p.66*) or simply some mixed leaves or steamed vegetables.

# Baked spinach scramble

Great for lunch or dinner, this dish also makes a delicious weekend breakfast dish – a new take on eggs florentine. Serves two.

ready in **20** minutes

2 tablespoons olive oil, plus extra for drizzling

2 slices wholegrain or rye bread, crumbled

½ teaspoon nutmeg

500g (1lb) spinach, washed and drained

Juice of 1 lemon

Juice of 1 orange

½ teaspoon cinnamon

Freshly ground black pepper

3 large eggs

60g (2oz) feta cheese, crumbled

Heat 1 tablespoon of the oil in a small pan, add the crumbs and nutmeg and stir-fry until crisp. Tip out of the pan on to kitchen paper to drain and set aside.

Lightly cook the spinach. Either steam it for a couple of minutes until the leaves have wilted, or put the wet leaves into a large pan and cook very gently, turning frequently, until wilted. Drain the spinach, then chop coarsely with scissors.

Heat the remaining oil in a heavy-based pan. Add the juices, cinnamon and black pepper, and stir everything together. Break in the eggs and stir well over a gentle heat to break up the eggs, until curds form. Quickly stir in the feta and the chopped spinach.

Turn the egg mixture into a shallow oven-proof dish, and top with the toasted breadcrumbs and a drizzle of olive oil. Brown under a medium grill for 2–3 minutes, then serve.

## SERVING IDEAS

**For lunch** A slice of toasted and buttered soda bread goes well with this dish.

**For dinner** Increase the quantity of spinach in this dish slightly, or add some kale for variety.

# Spicy chicken

Skinless chicken breasts are a great source of lean protein. These ideas give a tasty kick to a regular dish and are great for barbecues. To grind the spices use a traditional grinder, the coffee/nuts attachment of a blender, or a pestle and mortar. Each recipe serves two.

## Cajun-spiced chicken

**ready in 15 minutes**

2 skinless, boned chicken breasts (approx. 300g/10oz)

Olive oil

Lemon juice

**For the Cajun spice mix:**

½ teaspoon caraway seeds

½ teaspoon cumin seeds

1 teaspoon paprika

1 teaspoon cayenne or chilli pepper

½ teaspoon freshly ground black pepper

1 teaspoon dried oregano

First, prepare the spice mix. Grind the caraway and cumin seeds and mix with the other herbs and spices.

Rub the chicken breasts with a little olive oil and lemon juice, then coat them with the spice mix.

Put the chicken breasts in a grill pan and cook under a medium grill or over a medium heat on top of the stove for about 6 minutes each side, until cooked through but still juicy.

Slice the chicken breasts lengthways into four, then serve.

Cajun-spiced chicken

# Middle Eastern spicy chicken

ready in **15** minutes

2 skinless, boned chicken breasts
(approx. 300g/10oz)

Olive oil

Lemon juice

Sesame oil to drizzle

**For the Middle Eastern spice mix:**

3 teaspoons coriander seeds

6 teaspoons sesame seeds

3 teaspoons cumin seeds

Freshly ground black pepper

To dry-roast the coriander seeds put them in a heavy-based pan over a medium heat for 5–6 minutes, tossing occasionally to brown them on all sides and to prevent burning.

Put in a grinder, add the other spices and whizz to a powder.

Rub the chicken breasts with a little olive oil and lemon juice, then coat them with the spice mix.

Put the chicken breasts in a grill pan and cook under a medium grill or over a medium heat on top of the stove for about 6 minutes each side, until cooked through but still juicy.

Slice the chicken breasts lengthways into four. Drizzle with a little sesame oil and serve.

# Garam masala spicy chicken

ready in **15** minutes

2 skinless, boned chicken breasts
(approx. 300g/10oz)

Olive oil

Lemon juice

**For the garam masala spice mix:**

1 tablespoon cardamom pods

5cm (2in) piece whole cinnamon

1 teaspoon cumin seeds

1 teaspoon cloves

¼ of a nutmeg

Grind all the spices together. Rub the chicken breasts with a little olive oil and lemon juice, then coat them with the spice mix.

Put the chicken breasts in a grill pan and cook under a medium grill or over a medium heat on top of the stove for about 6 minutes each side, until cooked through but still juicy.

Slice the chicken breasts lengthways into four and serve.

# Indian spicy chicken

ready in **15** minutes

2 skinless, boned chicken breasts
(approx. 300g/10oz)

Olive oil

Lime juice

**For the Indian spice mix:**

1 tablespoon coriander seeds, dry-roasted (*see* Middle Eastern mix, *left*)

½ teaspoon chilli powder

½ teaspoon turmeric

Grind the roasted coriander seeds and mix with the chilli and turmeric.

Rub the chicken breasts with a little olive oil and lemon juice, then coat them with the spice mix.

Put the chicken breasts in a grill pan and cook under a medium grill or over a medium heat on top of the stove for about 6 minutes each side, until cooked through but still juicy.

Slice the chicken breasts lengthways into four. Drizzle with a little olive oil and serve.

## SERVING IDEAS

**For lunch** Any of these would work really well with a red or green salsa (*see p.94*) or with live natural yoghurt and a spoonful of rice.

**For dinner** Serve with green leaves, steamed vegetables, or one of the side-dishes on pp.96–97.

# Slow-burn side-dishes

These four dishes are called slow-burning due to their low GI rating, which means they provide steady energy and fill you up for quite a while yet don't trigger insulin production. Any left-overs are very tasty served cold, and if mashed or blended the three non-rice recipes also make great spreads for snacks. Each recipe serves two.

## Split yellow peas with spring onion

ready in **30** minutes

100g (3½oz) split yellow peas (or split mung beans or split red lentils)

300ml (½ pint) water

¼ teaspoon turmeric

1 tablespoon olive oil

1 tablespoon lemon juice

1 spring onion, trimmed and finely chopped

Freshly ground black pepper

Put the peas, water and turmeric in a saucepan. Bring to the boil, cover the pan, reduce the heat and simmer gently for 25 minutes until the peas are soft and the water has been absorbed. Add the olive oil, lemon juice, spring onion and black pepper, and stir well to combine the flavours before serving.

### SERVING IDEAS

**For lunch** Try a Mexican-style wrap (see p.104) of refried beans, pea mash (see p.66) or guacamole, and some rocket leaves.

**For dinner** These can liven up a simple poached chicken or omelette, or work well teamed with recipes such as the squash and feta rosti (see p.117)

## Butter beans Italian-style

ready in **20** minutes

1 x approx. 225g (7½oz) can butter beans, drained and rinsed

150ml (¼ pint) vegetable stock (see p.149)

1 tablespoon olive oil

1 garlic clove, finely chopped

1 heaped tablespoon tomato purée

Freshly ground black pepper

1 tablespoon chopped fresh parsley, to garnish

Put the butter beans in a heavy-based saucepan and add the hot stock. Bring to the boil and simmer gently to heat the beans thoroughly.

In a separate pan, heat the oil, add the garlic and stir-fry for a minute or two, then add the tomato purée, black pepper and 3 tablespoons of stock from the pan of beans. Mix well over a very low heat.

Drain the beans from the stock and add them to the pan of tomato mixture. Stir well to combine the ingredients and serve with the parsley scattered over the top.

## Refried beans

ready in **30** minutes

1 tablespoon olive oil

½ onion (approx. 60g/2oz)

1 garlic clove, crushed

½ teaspoon cumin seeds

1 x approx. 250g (8oz) can mixed beans, drained and rinsed

1 x 225g (7½oz) can chopped tomatoes

¼ teaspoon chilli powder

Freshly ground black pepper

Heat the oil in a heavy-based saucepan and add the onion, garlic and cumin seeds. Cook gently until the onions are soft and beginning to colour. Add the beans, tomatoes, chilli powder and black pepper. Cook gently for 10–15 minutes, stirring and gently mashing down the beans with a fork. When the mixture is thick and beginning to come away from the sides of the pan, remove from the heat.

About 10 minutes before you are ready to serve the beans, heat a drizzle of olive oil in a small non-stick frying pan. Add the bean mix and flatten down into a "cake". Cook for 5 minutes over a medium-high heat, to brown the base. Drizzle the top with a little more olive oil and slip the pan under a hot grill for another 2–3 minutes to cook the top. Slide the bean "cake" on to a flat plate, cut in half and serve.

# Spiced rice

| ready in **30** minutes |

100g (3½oz) brown basmati rice

1 tablespoon olive oil

2 whole cardamom pods

1cm (½in) piece cinnamon stick

2 whole cloves

½ onion (approx. 45g/1½oz), finely chopped

250ml (8fl oz) vegetable stock (*see p.149*)

Rinse the rice in a colander, put it in a bowl of fresh water and leave to stand until you are ready to use it.

Heat the oil in a heavy-based saucepan and add the spices whole. Stir them once or twice in the oil, then add the onions. Stir-fry until the onion begins to brown.

Drain the rice thoroughly and add it to the pan. Stir the mixture to coat the rice with oil before adding the hot stock. Bring to the boil, cover the pan, reduce the heat and simmer for 25 minutes, or until the rice is cooked. If all the stock has not been absorbed, turn up the heat and boil away the remainder before serving.

Split yellow peas with spring onion

Butter beans Italian-style

Refried beans

Spiced rice

# Menu ideas

# Meals in store

Be prepared. With just a few tins and dried goods you have the staples for some filling, healthy dishes that will prevent you from making a poor food choice when you have had no time to shop recently.

## Quick kedgeree

*Make this dish with these ingredients:*

- **fish**  half a can of tuna, mackerel or salmon, plus a few chopped anchovies
  and
- **egg**  one hard-boiled egg
  and
- **vegetables**  a handful of frozen sweetcorn and a pinch of cumin
  and
- **brown rice or quinoa**  a portion of brown rice if lunch-time, or quinoa if dinner-time (if using quinoa, increase the proportion of vegetables)

## Tuna and mixed-bean salad

*Make this salad with these ingredients:*

- **fish**  half a can of tuna, mackerel or salmon
  and
- **beans**  half a can of mixed beans, such as borlotti, kidney or butter beans
  and
- **vegetables**  a handful of frozen peas, sweetcorn or broad beans
  and (if lunch-time)
- **quinoa**  one portion of quinoa, couscous or bulgar wheat

## Vegetable soup

*Make this soup into a balanced meal with these ingredients:*

- **soup**  one can of vegetable-based soup, such as carrot, tomato or pumpkin
  and
- **pulses**  half a can of chick-peas, lentils, cannellini or black-eye beans
  and (if lunch-time)
- **bread**  one thick slice of wholemeal or rye bread

Vegetable soup        Omelette

Tuna and mixed-bean salad

## Vegetable chilli

*Make this filling chilli with these ingredients:*

- **quick tomato sauce**  half a portion of tomato sauce (*see p.143*) or ratatouille (*see p.96*)

  and

- **beans**  half a tin of red kidney beans, or black-eye or borlotti beans

  and

- **flavours and spices**  one onion, chopped, and some chilli powder

  and (if lunch-time)

- **brown rice**  a portion of brown rice

## Quick ragoût

*Make this hearty dish with these ingredients:*

- **ratatouille**  half a portion of ratatouille (*see p.96*), or half a can

  and

- **flavours and spices**  one chopped onion and some dried herbs

  and

- **goat's cheese or prawns**  a palm-sized piece of soft or hard goat's cheese, crumbled, or just under a handful of frozen prawns

  and (if lunch-time)

- **pasta**  a portion of corn, buckwheat or wholewheat pasta

## Omelette

*Make this quick omelette with these ingredients:*

- **eggs**  two eggs

  and

- **vegetables**  a teaspoon of pesto mixed with half a tin of chopped plum tomatoes or half a jar of roasted sweet peppers, chopped

  or

- **beans**  half a tin of mixed beans, such as flageleot, cannellini, borlotti or black-eye beans

# Pasta and pesto

This dish's carbohydrate/protein balance means that it is best served at lunch-time. If you prefer, make it with 125g (4oz) quinoa cooked in stock in place of the pasta. Serves two.

**ready in 20 minutes**

125g (4oz) buckwheat noodles, or other pasta

2 eggs

Pinch of mixed herbs

3 tablespoons pesto (*see p.69*)

10 sun-dried tomatoes in oil, drained and sliced into ribbons

Freshly ground black pepper

Cook the pasta according to the instructions on the packet. When cooked, drain through a colander and tip back into the empty pan to keep warm.

While the pasta is cooking, make a flat omelette with the eggs, flavoured with mixed herbs (*see Egg ribbons with cumin rice, p.139*). When the omelette is cooked, leave to cool, then roll up and cut into ribbons about ½cm (¼in) wide.

Stir the pesto into the pasta, add the tomatoes and black pepper, and serve with the egg ribbons on top.

# Chick-pea and ratatouille stew

This stew makes a filling meal on its own, and is delicious served either hot or cold. Any left-overs can be blended or mashed if you want to make a smooth, healthy dip. Serves two.

ready in **10** minutes

1 tablespoon olive oil

1 small onion, sliced

1 x approx. 400g (13oz) can ratatouille, or equivalent amount of home-made ratatouille (*see p.96*)

1 x approx. 400g (13oz) can chick-peas, drained and rinsed

Juice of 1 lemon

1 teaspoon paprika (or smoked paprika, if available)

Heat the oil in a heavy-based saucepan, add the onion and cook gently until it begins to soften and turn opaque. Add the ratatouille, mix well and heat through for a few minutes. Add the chick-peas, lemon juice and paprika. Simmer everything together for a few more minutes to warm it through, then serve.

## SERVING IDEAS

**For lunch** Serve with a slice of wholemeal bread or some brown rice.

**For dinner** Stir in some frozen spinach or broad beans to boost the complex carbohydrate ratio.

# Tuna and mixed-bean salad

LUNCH OR DINNER

This salad can be made very quickly using ingredients from the storecupboard, with fresh herbs and cucumber added if you have any. Serves two.

**ready in 10 minutes**

2 tablespoons olive oil

1 tablespoon lemon juice

1 tablespoon water

1 teaspoon tomato purée

1 teaspoon soy sauce

1 teaspoon Thai fish sauce (optional)

1 x 400g (13oz) can mixed beans, drained and rinsed

1 x 200g (7oz) can tuna in spring water, drained and broken into chunks

½ small red onion, finely sliced

½ small cucumber, diced (optional)

Fresh green herbs, such as parsley, coriander or marjoram, to garnish (optional)

Put the olive oil, lemon juice, water, tomato purée, soy sauce and fish sauce in a salad bowl and mix together with a fork. Mix in the beans, then fold in the tuna chunks carefully so that they do not break up even further. Top with the raw onion.

Cucumber adds a refreshing coolness to this salad so, if you have any, add small cubes of it to the salad before the tuna. Garnish with freshly chopped herbs if they are available.

## SERVING IDEAS

**For lunch** Add a spoonful of brown rice or bulgar wheat.

**For dinner** If you have any salad vegetables, such as tomatoes, celery or sweet peppers, chop a few and add them with the tuna.

# Egg ribbons with cumin rice

This lunch is simple to prepare and extremely versatile. If you don't have eggs available, try substituting chicken strips, canned fish or smoked mackerel, for instance. Serves two.

**ready in 30 minutes**

**SERVING IDEA**

**For lunch** If you have any green salad leaves in the fridge, serve them on the side drizzled with balsamic vinegar.

1 teaspoon olive oil
1 small onion (approx. 100g/3½oz), chopped
1 teaspoon cumin seeds
150g (5oz) brown rice
350ml (12fl oz) vegetable stock (*see p.149*)
2 eggs
Mixed herbs or spices (whatever you have in the cupboard)
Freshly ground black pepper
8 sun-dried tomatoes in oil, cut into strips
Chopped fresh parsley (optional)

Heat the olive oil in a saucepan, add the onion and cook gently until soft but not coloured. Add the cumin and stir for 1 minute. Add the rice, stir to coat with the oil, then pour in the hot stock. Cover the pan, bring to the boil, reduce the heat and simmer for 30 minutes, until the stock is absorbed and the rice tender.

Beat the eggs in a bowl, and add a good pinch of any dried herbs or spices you may have and some black pepper. Wipe the inside of an omelette pan or small frying pan with a little oil, heat the pan and pour in the egg mixture. Cook the egg mixture quite quickly, without stirring it, to make a flat omelette. Tip out of the pan and set aside to cool. When the omelette is cool, roll it up and cut into strips ½cm (¼in) wide.

Stir the tomatoes and egg ribbons into the rice and serve garnished with parsley, if you have some.

# Omelette with beans

This filling omelette is based on storecupboard ingredients and is quick to make. If you don't have a can of beans, try crumbling in some goat's cheese or some canned fish. Serves two.

**ready in 10 minutes**

4 eggs

2 heaped teaspoons Dijon mustard

1 teaspoon dried mixed herbs

Freshly ground black pepper

1 x 200g (7oz) can chopped tomatoes

Spray of olive oil

½ x 400g (7oz) can flageleot or cannellini beans, drained and rinsed

### SERVING IDEAS

**For lunch** Keep the preparation time to a minimum by serving with a thick slice of wholemeal or rye bread and a few salad leaves.

**For dinner** Serve with a few steamed peas or mangetout or any green vegetables available.

Break the eggs into a bowl and whisk them with the mustard, dried herbs and black pepper. Mix in the chopped tomatoes.

Heat a non-stick omelette pan or small frying pan and spray lightly with olive oil. Pour in the egg mixture,

spreading it evenly over the base of the pan. Scatter the beans over the top and cook until the bottom is set and turning golden. Put the pan under a hot grill for 3–4 minutes until the top is just set and golden in colour, then serve.

# Lentils with onion and tomatoes

LUNCH OR DINNER

Cut down on the preparation time by using canned Puy lentils, if available, or green lentils as in the lemony spinach soup (*see p.88*). All varieties of lentils are a great source of protein. Serves two.

**ready in 30 minutes**

150g (5oz) Puy lentils

Approx. 300ml (½ pint) vegetable stock (*see p.149*)

1 tablespoon olive oil

1 onion, finely sliced

1 garlic clove, chopped

1 x 225g (7½oz) can chopped tomatoes

1 heaped teaspoon tomato purée

1 teaspoon dried mixed herbs

Juice of ½ lemon

Place the lentils in a heavy-based saucepan and pour in enough vegetable stock to cover them well. Bring to the boil, cover the pan, reduce the heat and simmer for about 25 minutes, or until the lentils are cooked. Check the liquid level from time to time and add more hot stock if necessary. Drain the cooked lentils.

While the lentils are cooking, heat the oil in a heavy-based pan, add the onion and garlic and cook until softened and golden. Add the tomatoes and their juice, tomato purée and dried herbs to the pan, mix well and bring to simmering point. Stir the lentils and lemon juice into the onion and tomato mixture and serve.

## SERVING IDEAS

**For lunch** Serve with a spoonful of brown rice or a few boiled potatoes drizzled with olive oil.

**For dinner** Stir in some frozen spinach or green beans.

# With just a can of tomatoes ...

Here are four great recipes, all with a can of tomatoes as their main ingredient. They are the perfect answer to the dilemma of a nearly-bare cupboard. The quick tomato sauce is excellent with grilled chicken or fish and will keep for several days in a sealed container in the fridge. Each recipe serves two.

## Baked eggs on tomatoes and peppers

ready in **25** minutes

3 tablespoons olive oil

1 onion (approx. 200g/7oz), coarsely chopped

1 garlic clove, crushed and chopped

1 red pepper, cored, deseeded and chopped

1 yellow pepper, cored, deseeded and chopped

1 x 400g (13oz) can chopped tomatoes

2–3 tablespoons chopped fresh parsley

Freshly ground black pepper

2 eggs

Pre-heat the oven to 180°C/350°F/gas mark 4.

Heat the oil in a heavy-based saucepan. Add the onion and garlic and cook for about 3 minutes until transparent. Add the peppers and cook for a further 5 minutes, until they begin to soften. Add the tomatoes, parsley and black pepper and simmer everything together for a further 5 minutes, stirring often.

When the mixture is cooked, pour into an ovenproof dish, break the eggs on top and bake for about 10 minutes, or until the egg whites are just set. Serve immediately.

## Quick tomato soup

ready in **10** minutes

1 x recipe quantity quick tomato sauce (*see opposite*)

300ml (½ pint) vegetable stock (*see p.149*)

1 tablespoon live natural yoghurt

Fresh basil, to garnish

Put the quick tomato sauce and stock in a blender and blend to make a soup.

Pour into a saucepan and heat to simmering point. Divide between two bowls and put a swirl of yoghurt on top of each. Serve garnished with the basil.

Baked eggs on tomatoes and peppers

# Tomato and lime juice drink

ready in **5** minutes

1 x 400g (13oz) can tomatoes

Juice of 1 lime

Dash of Worcestershire sauce

Put all the ingredients in a blender and blend thoroughly to make a zesty and refreshing tomato drink.

Note: A measure of vodka turns this tomato drink into a cocktail very like the famous Bloody Mary.

# Quick tomato sauce

ready in **20** minutes

2 tablespoons olive oil

1 onion (approx. 150g/5oz), finely chopped

1 garlic clove, finely chopped

1 x 200g (7oz) can chopped tomatoes

1 tablespoon lemon juice

1 tablespoon tomato purée

Freshly ground black pepper

2 tablespoons chopped fresh herbs, such as parsley, coriander or basil

Heat the oil in a heavy-based saucepan and add the onion and garlic. Cook gently for about 5 minutes, until softened but not coloured. Add the tomatoes, lemon juice, tomato purée and black pepper, bring to the boil and simmer for 10–15 minutes, until the sauce has thickened. Stir in the chopped fresh herbs.

Tomato and lime juice drink

SERVING IDEAS

**For lunch** The soup makes a great lunch, hot or cold, accompanied by some wholemeal bread. Add some pulses, cubed tofu, smoked mackerel or chicken strips to provide the protein.

**For dinner** The baked eggs recipe is a meal in itself. Or, use a few spoonfuls of the quick tomato sauce to liven up a chicken breast or fish fillet with some steamed vegetables.

# Eating out

If you have a mantra for eating out, whether at a restaurant, a friend's house, a work function or even on holiday, then it should be "Where's the protein?". Keep that in mind, and remember the 10 principles, and you can navigate any situation.

There are many strategies to ensure that, whatever the occasion, you won't need to sabotage your weight control to enjoy it. Simple tactics such as drinking a few glasses of water and having a little snack before you go out, for example, will ensure that you avoid hunger and blood-glucose lows.

## Think strong
Sometimes a slight shift in mindset is involved. If you've been brought up to eat everything on your plate, for instance, adjust to leaving food. If portion sizes are enormous, you can gauge how much to eat using your hands, so leave any excess.

Don't feel intimidated about making requests in restaurants, too: if you want extra green vegetables instead of the potato mash your dish is served with, just ask. Sauces and dressings can be served separately, keeping you in control of how much you eat. The current allergy-aware climate is becoming more and more receptive to individual requirements.

You might want to indulge in "stealth-dieting" – don't actually tell anyone you're watching what you eat, and then you'll be spared the I-know-better advice, the conspiratorial leading-you-astray, and the evenings spent discussing every diet someone's mother/neighbour/sister has done and how well/badly it worked for them.

## Where there's a will ...
Desserts are a problem, so you will need a little willpower here, or apply the 80:20 rule (*see pp.12–13*). And don't be tempted to skip a meal earlier in the day to "save" the calories for your evening out – it doesn't work that way and will upset your blood-glucose levels (*see pp.16–17*).

### DRINKING AND DIETING

Alcohol is a simple carbohydrate that is easily absorbed into the blood, raising levels of blood-glucose quite quickly and probably sending you over the insulin threshold. Therefore I suggest you drink alcohol only with your meal, not before, as the presence of food will slow down the glucose conversion to some extent. I know from my own experience that a couple of drinks before dinner may be part of the whole evening, but your chances of making good food choices afterwards are decreased as you feel more relaxed. This doesn't mean you have to abstain, just be aware.

# Hosting a dinner party

If you're hosting the dinner, you're in control, which is perfect. I believe that it is entirely possible to feed your guests from The Food Doctor Everyday Diet without any of them realising they're on your "diet" with you.

For example, start with a soup, or crudités with dips (perhaps have these for people to graze on beforehand – then you won't feel obliged to offer crisps). Your main course could be almost any recipe from this book, such as the seared tuna with cinnamon (*see p.128*), or the chicken with summer herbs (*see p.123*). Serve with vegetables, salads or mashes and guests won't even notice the absence of starchy carbohydrates. If you want, of course, you can serve these up, but simply abstain yourself unless it's lunch-time. Dessert is less easy, as you don't want to be eating sugary food: perhaps a very dark chocolate mousse that has little added sugar; or a fresh fruit salad with yoghurt rather than cream; or serve cheese – just avoid the crackers yourself.

If you present dishes in separate serving bowls, your guests can help themselves to what they want, and you can stick to The Food Doctor plan easily and without fuss.

# Dining out at a friend's

This can be slightly tricky, as you are not in control of the cooking. You are unable to control at what time you will eat, so I suggest having a small snack before you leave the house, even if it's just a rice cake with a protein spread, or some vegetables and houmous or fish dip.

You can't dictate what you are served, either, but you can control what you actually eat. Usually somewhere within whatever is served there will be a protein and some vegetables together with the necessary complex carbohydrates. You have the tools to assess and create a suitable meal from what you are served up: the food group ratios, the portion sizes according to your hand size, and the mantra "Where's the protein?". Leave what doesn't suit you on the side of your plate – whoever is providing the food won't be offended. If they ask why you didn't eat whatever it is you have left, just say that you are full, and have eaten enough.

If, unfortunately, you have been offered a main course based on simple carbohydrates (such as a risotto), or you feel that you want to eat more than usual or eat in a way that wouldn't fit in with my plan, then be honest with yourself about it and do not feel guilty. See this as a "20 per cent moment" (*see pp.12–13*) – you have made good food choices for 80 per cent of the time, so you can relax the rules for 20 per cent. Assuming you don't do it every day, you won't suddenly regain the weight you have lost.

# Restaurants

The great thing about eating in restaurants is that you can order what you want from the menu, as long as you bear the 10 principles in mind. If you think about what type of food is on offer, then I am sure you can apply the principles almost anywhere (*see box, opposite*).

Whether you eat out because your job demands it, or your partner loves it, or because you choose to, it's really easy to follow The Food Doctor plan. I have to eat out a fair amount, and find it simple to follow my own principles – I don't have any special willpower, or self-control, just the confidence to eat in a way that suits me.

When sizing up the menu, remember the mantra "Where's the protein?". If there isn't any, then the dish is unlikely to suit you. Don't be afraid to be specific about what you want to eat – you're the customer, remember. And, of course, avoid the bread basket.

# Drinks parties

This is tricky for healthy eating, not just due to the alcohol intake, the empty stomach, and the likelihood of poor food choices following later in the evening. An average evening of drinks, possibly with nibbles, followed by a late meal, plays havoc with your blood-glucose levels and insulin production is pretty much inevitable.

Minimise the dangers by drinking plenty of water before you go out, and eating a small snack (*see pp.62–63*) to steady your blood-glucose levels. Try to avoid nibbles such as crisps and salted nuts, sticking to olives or raw, unsalted nuts if you can. Stick to white or red wine rather than spirits, beers or lager, which have higher GI scores.

# Holidays

Traditional dieters all too often lose weight before a holiday so they feel comfortable in their bikinis or swimming gear. Sadly, once the holiday feeling kicks in, we all know that we can abandon our good intentions and eat and eat and eat (I bet there will be someone who says "Go on, you're on holiday, you deserve it – after all, look how good you have been").

Remind yourself that it's the holiday you deserve, not weight gain, so follow the 10 principles and you will be fine. By all means have fun and try new foods, but you will be back on the diet treadmill if you just over-eat and then have to diet again once you are home.

## DIFFERENT RESTAURANTS, DIFFERENT CUISINES, SAME TACTICS

In almost any type of restaurant, there will be something on the menu to fit the 10 principles. Do remember portion control too.

### FRENCH RESTAURANTS

French food is easy – onion soup and a grilled piece of fish or meat, with some potatoes and vegetables is typical, and certainly what I would order. The trick is to feel free to ask for just a couple of new potatoes, rather than let the restaurant choose the portion size for you.

### ITALIAN RESTAURANTS

You don't have to have pasta or a pizza, as even the most basic pizza chain will have salads on offer. You could start with a mozzarella and tomato salad, followed by seafood pasta. Or grilled veal with vegetables. The protein doesn't have to be in both the starter and the main course, just consider how much protein you are eating in the whole meal. This means that if you want some bread at the start of the meal, then this counts as part of your carbohydrate intake. If you choose pasta, then ask for extra seafood and less pasta – restaurants are there to serve food, so never be afraid to ask for what you want.

### INDIAN RESTAURANTS

Indian food is overly dependent on carbohydrates so you must be especially aware at an Indian restaurant. The typical meal starts with papadums, which are made from lentil flour. This contains protein, but only a little, so papadums hardly count towards your protein quota. Your typical order might previously have been a chicken dish with a sauce, some naan bread and some rice. If you follow The Food Doctor plan and apply the 10 principles, then you can still start with the papadums, but follow them instead with tandoori chicken or fish, accompanied by vegetables, and a lentil or chick-pea dish.

### ASIAN RESTAURANTS

Asian food is often heavy on rice and noodles, but that doesn't mean you have to avoid this cuisine altogether. You could order chicken satay to start, then have a duck or tofu curry and some rice. However, ask for extra chicken (make a fuss if you have to), and share one order of rice with someone else. This way you can still achieve 40 per cent protein while enjoying the meal.

### MEXICAN RESTAURANTS

This cuisine is very carbohydrate-focused so do ensure you eat something before you arrive at the restaurant. Have a few corn chips, then try some chicken or beef tacos or enchiladas with a side-salad to achieve the ideal ratio of protein to carbohydrates.

# Useful recipes and ingredients

## Five-spice paste

Five-spice paste is a little easier to use than powder (*see below*), because it can be blended easily. If neither the powder nor the paste is available, you could substitute a small pinch of cinnamon and clove to the dish you are cooking, although it will not taste quite the same.

2 tablespoons five-spice powder

1 tablespoon soy sauce

2 garlic cloves, crushed

Blend all the ingredients to a paste. It can be stored for up to a week in a screw-topped jar in the fridge

## Five-spice powder

This seasoning originated in China and takes its name from the five flavours included in it (salty, sour, bitter, pungent and sweet). Sometimes it can be extended to seven with the addition of cardamom, dried ginger, or liquorice. Both the powder and paste (*see above*) are quite pungent so use sparingly.

6 star anise

1 tablespoon Szechuan pepper

1 tablespoon ground fennel seeds

2 teaspoons cloves

2 teaspoons ground cassia or cinnamon

Grind all the ingredients in a blender until very fine. Sieve and store in an airtight container.

## Green tapenade

Tapenade is a spread or accompaniment from southern France. This recipe is based on green olives, but black olives can be used if that's what you have available.

150g (5oz) green olives, pitted and finely chopped

6–7 anchovy fillets, rinsed and dried

Scant tablespoon capers

Olive oil

Lemon juice

Put the olives, anchovies and capers in a bowl and mash them well together. Add a dash of olive oil and a few drops of lemon juice to taste. Store in the fridge in a screw-topped jar.

## Herbes de Provence

The herbs in the mixture vary considerably, but usually include four or five of the following: sage, parsley, rosemary, hyssop, thyme, marjoram, fennel seed, savory and bay, plus basil and lavender. Vary the amounts and herb choices to suit your own taste.

3 tablespoons dried thyme

2 tablespoons dried marjoram

1 teaspoon dried rosemary

1 tablespoon dried savory

1 teaspoon dried lavender flowers

Crumble or grind the herbs and store in an air-tight jar for 2–3 months.

## Horseradish sauce

An often-used, quickly made substitute for bought horseradish sauce is a mixture of finely grated fresh horseradish and soured cream, or cream and a little lemon juice or vinegar. This sauce is commonly used for fish or poultry, or of vegetables such as courgettes or beetroot. Makes enough sauce for four servings.

125g (4oz) live natural yoghurt

2 tablespoons horseradish, freshly grated

2 tablespoons chopped fresh dill

Freshly ground black pepper

Mix all the ingredients together in a bowl. Store, covered, in the fridge until needed.

If you wish to serve it warm, heat it over a bain marie but ensure it doesn't boil because this will make it curdle.

## Soy sauce

Soy sauce is extracted from boiled soya beans that have been fermented with barley or wheat, then salted and fermented again. Choose a light sauce if possible for use in cooking, ideally in combination with other liquids such as wine or stock, and a dark sauce for a condiment to be sprinkled sparingly (it is very salty) over finished dishes.

## Stock, fish

To make a good fish stock ask the fishmonger for trimmings – the heads without gills, fins and bones – of white fish such as monkfish, cod, whiting and, because their bones are full of gelatine, turbot and sole. Avoid oily fish like mackerel and herring. Makes approximately 2 litres (3½ pints).

1–1½kg (2–3lb) white fish trimmings

1 onion, peeled and sliced

1 carrot, sliced

1 small leek (white part only), sliced

1 stick celery, chopped

Sprig of dill

Sprig of parsley

1 bay leaf

10–12 black peppercorns

450ml (¾ pint) dry white wine

2 litres (3 pints) water

Put all the ingredients in a large saucepan and bring slowly to the boil, skimming the surface until the liquid is clear. As soon as the stock has reached boiling point, turn down the heat, partially cover the pan and simmer for 30 minutes. Do not let the stock boil and do not simmer it for more than the 30 minutes, or it will become sticky.

Immediately strain the stock through a muslin-lined colander or sieve. The stock may be used at once or cooled and stored in the fridge for one day only before using it. Try freezing stock in an ice-cube tray so that you have convenient portions that you can add to smaller dishes.

## Stock, vegetable

Most root vegetables, onions, leeks and celery are all good basics for a vegetable stock. Avoid strong green vegetables such as cabbage, broccoli, spinach or Brussels sprouts as they give stock too strong a flavour and colour. The whole garlic bulb in this stock may sound a lot, but it adds a deliciously subtle flavour. Makes approximately 1.5 litres (2½ pints). It can be frozen in handy portion sizes when it has cooled.

2 potatoes or 1 parsnip, roughly chopped

2 carrots, roughly chopped

1 large onion, quartered

1 stick celery, roughly chopped

1 garlic bulb, unpeeled (optional)

1 bay leaf

Large sprig fresh thyme or ½ teaspoon dried thyme

Large sprig parsley

6–8 black peppercorns

2 litres (3½ pints) water

Put all the ingredients into a large saucepan. Bring slowly to the boil, then reduce the heat, partly cover and simmer gently for about 2 hours.

While the stock is simmering, line a colander or large sieve with a piece of muslin and set it over a large bowl. When the stock has finished cooking, pour it through the muslin-lined colander into the bowl. Discard the contents of the colander. Cover the bowl and set aside to cool thoroughly before storing in the refrigerator. It will keep for 3–4 days in the refrigerator, or you can freeze it.

## Tamarind paste

Tamarind pods look like long dates and the pulp inside, which has a distinctive sour, fruity flavour, is used as a souring agent in Indian and South-east Asian cookery. Tamarind is usually found in the form of a paste. If it is not available, use lemon juice or wine vinegar instead.

## Thai fish sauce

Often labelled simply "fish sauce" it is sold in the Oriental foods section in the supermarket. Thai fish sauce is a very salty, thin, brown liquid used in Malay and Thai cooking, where it is called "nam pla".

It is made by fermenting fish or shrimps with salt and soy. The liquid that is drained off from the fermentation is the fish sauce. If it is not available, anchovy essence makes an acceptable substitute.

## Tofu

This ingredient of Chinese and Japanese cooking is made from puréed soy beans. Bean curd is soft and white, with a cheese-like texture that ranges from firm to silken. It is high in protein and very low in fat.

Firm tofu is used largely as a salad ingredient, added in bite-sized cubes. Silken tofu is the best tofu for cooking. It is used largely for blending with other ingredients to make sauces.

Tofu is also available marinated or smoked. These are best used in salads or stir-fries.

# Smart food choices

These charts give you a simple overview to help you make the best possible food choices. They are based on a range of criteria, including antioxidant properties, levels of essential fatty acids, fibre content and rating on the Glycaemic Index (GI).

The GI rating is, in effect, a measure of the sugar content of carbohydrates and a guide to how quickly the body converts that sugar to glucose. The quicker the conversion, the higher the GI score. Carbohydrates fall into two categories: simple and complex. Simple carbohydrates have had their fibre removed, while the fibre of complex carbohydrates remains intact. Fibre helps slow down the process of converting food into glucose, so foods high in fibre have lower GI scores. Foods high in sugars and low in fibre convert rapidly into blood-glucose and therefore have relatively high GI scores.

## Protein profiles

| | MEAT & POULTRY | |
|---|---|---|
| **Ideal choice**<br>These foods are all complete proteins and are therefore the best choice. | Calves' liver<br>Chicken, skinless<br>Lambs' liver<br>Turkey, skinless<br>Veal | |
| **Good choice**<br>You can include these food choices frequently as part of a healthy diet. | | |
| **Adequate choice**<br>Eat these foods occasionally. | Bacon<br>Beef<br>Duck, skinless<br>Game<br>Ham | Lamb<br>Mince<br>Offal<br>Pork |

## Carbohydrate profiles

| | GRAIN-BASED FOODS | FRUITS | |
|---|---|---|---|
| **Ideal choice**<br>The complex carbohydrates at this level are ideal choices because they supply high levels of energy for a sustained period. They are all broken down slowly into glucose by the body so they have a low GI score. | Barley flakes<br>Bran flakes<br>Buckwheat flour or flakes<br>Millet<br>Oatmeal or oat flakes<br>Rye bread (wholegrain) or rye flakes | Apples<br>Apricots (fresh)<br>Blackberries<br>Blackcurrants<br>Cranberries<br>Grapefruit<br>Lemons<br>Limes<br>Pears | Plums<br>Redcurrants<br>Strawberries |
| **Good choice**<br>The foods in this category have a medium GI score and so they provide reasonably good levels of energy at a fairly steady rate. | Couscous<br>Granola bars containing nuts<br>Pasta, e.g. corn, buckwheat or wholewheat<br>Pumpernickel bread<br>Rice, brown<br>Wholemeal bread | Blueberries<br>Cherries<br>Grapes, white or<br>red<br>Loganberries<br>Mandarins<br>Mangoes | Oranges<br>Papayas<br>Peaches<br>Pineapple<br>Satsumas<br>Tangerines |
| **Adequate choice**<br>These foods have a relatively high GI score and provide only short-term energy, so do not include them too frequently in your eating plan. | Bagels<br>Breadsticks<br>Breakfast cereals (unsweetened)<br>French bread<br>Soda bread<br>Sourdough bread | Bananas<br>Dried fruit<br>Figs<br>Prunes | |

| DAIRY | VEGETARIAN | FISH | | | |
|-------|------------|------|---|---|---|
| Duck eggs<br>Hens' eggs<br>Quails' eggs | Nuts (raw)<br>Quinoa<br>Quorn<br>Pulses, e.g. cannellini<br>  beans, butter beans,<br>  chick-peas, lentils<br>Seeds, e.g. pumpkin,<br>  sesame and sunflower<br>Tofu | Anchovies<br>Bluefish*<br>Bream<br>Brill<br>Carp*<br>Cod<br>Dover sole<br>Eel*<br>Grey Mullet* | Gurnard<br>Haddock<br>Hake<br>Halibut*<br>Herring*<br>Hoki<br>Lemon sole<br>Mackerel*<br>Mahi Mahi* | Marlin*<br>Monkfish<br>Orange roughy<br>Perch*<br>Plaice<br>Red mullet*<br>Salmon*<br>Sardine*<br>Sea bass | Sea bream<br>Skate<br>Sprat*<br>Swordfish*<br>Trout*<br>Tuna*<br>Turbot<br>Whitebait*<br>Whiting |
| Cottage cheese, low-fat<br>Goat's cheese (hard or<br>  soft)<br>Yoghurt, live natural<br>  low-fat | Baked beans<br>(unsweetened) | Langoustines<br>Lobster<br>Mussels<br>Prawns<br>Scallops<br>Squid | | | |
| Butter, unsalted<br>Cheese, hard<br>Fromage frais<br>Milk, whole or semi-<br>  skimmed<br>Ricotta cheese<br>Yoghurt, full-fat | | | | | |

*Also a good source of omega-3 fats

| COOKED VEGETABLES | | RAW FOODS | | DRINKS |
|-------------------|---|-----------|---|--------|
| Artichokes<br>Asparagus<br>Beans, e.g. broad,<br>  green, runner<br>Broccoli<br>Brussels sprouts<br>Cabbage, red or<br>  green<br>Cauliflower | Greens<br>Kale<br>Leeks<br>Pak choi<br>Peppers, red,<br>  orange or yellow<br>Onions<br>Spinach | Bean-sprouts<br>Celery<br>Chicory<br>Lamb's lettuce<br>Mushrooms<br>Peppers, red,<br>  orange or yellow<br>Rocket<br>Spinach | Sprouted seeds<br>  and beans, e.g.<br>  alfalfa, mung<br>Tomatoes<br>Watercress | Vegetable juice |
| Carrots<br>Courgettes<br>Kidney beans<br>Marrow<br>Pumpkin<br>Turnips<br>Yellow squash | | Avocados<br>Beetroot<br>Carrots<br>Celeriac<br>Olives<br>Peppers, green<br>Radishes | | Fruit juice |
| Aubergines<br>Parsnips<br>Peas<br>Potatoes (baked,<br>  boiled, mashed)<br>Squash | Sweet potatoes<br>Yams | | | Beer<br>Mixers<br>Spirits<br>Wine |

# Glossary

**Adrenaline**
A hormone secreted by the adrenal glands (located above the kidneys) in response to low blood-glucose levels, exercise or stress. Adrenaline causes an increase in blood-glucose levels by breaking down glycogen stores to glucose in the liver. It enncourages the release of fatty acids from body tissue, causes blood vessels to dilate and increases cardiac output.

**Amino acids**
Amino acids form the basic constituents of proteins. There are nine essential amino acids that cannot be produced by the body and must be supplied by food, although the ninth is only considered essential for children.

**Blood-glucose levels**
The concentration of glucose in the blood.

**Cardiovascular**
Relating to the heart and blood vessels.

**Complex carbohydrate**
A food containing insoluble fibre, which helps to slow down the process of digestion.

**Diuretic**
Increases the rate of urination, generally decreasing water retention.

**Essential fats**
Fats that are essential to the normal functioning of the body, but which cannot be created by the body and so have to be derived from foods. Omega-3 essential fats are found in oily fish, such as salmon, mackerel, herring, tuna and sardines, and also in flax and hemp seeds. Omega-6 oils are found in most seeds and nuts except peanuts.

**Famine mode**
The point at which a dieter's metabolism senses a reduction in food intake and slows down to conserve energy in response to this "famine" situation.

**Fibre**
Mostly derived from plant cell walls, fibre is not broken down by digestive enzymes but may be partly digested by beneficial bacteria in the gut. Fibre is essential for good digestive health: insoluble fibre provides bulk to the faeces and so helps to prevent constipation; soluble fibre helps to reduce blood-cholesterol levels and eliminate toxins and excess hormones.

**Free radical**
A naturally occurring, short-lived, highly unstable molecule that is usually produced when chemical reactions occur in the body. In its search for stability it will "steal" an electron from another molecule, causing it to become a free radical. This results in a cascade of free radical activity, which can result in the deterioration of tissue and degeneration associated with ageing, cancer, Alzheimer's, Parkinson's disease, arthritis, and many others. Stress, pollution, poor diet, excessive sun exposure, smoking, radiation and illness all increase the build-up of free radicals.

**Glucose**
A simple form of sugar, also known as a monosaccharide. It occurs naturally in various foods – for example, in some fruits – and is the body's main source of fuel. Carbohydrates are broken down into glucose by the body. However, body cells cannot use glucose without the help of insulin.

**Gluten**
An insoluble protein group that is found in wheat, rye, barley and oats. Gluten is the mixture of proteins, which includes gliadin, to which coeliacs are intolerant.

**Glycaemic index**
The glycaemic index (GI) ranks foods on a scale of 1–100 according to how they affect blood-glucose levels. It measures how much blood-glucose

increases in the two or three hours after eating. Foods that are broken down quickly during the process of digestion have the highest GI values (70 and above) – they make blood-glucose levels rise high quickly. Foods that are broken down slowly, releasing glucose gradually into the bloodstream, have low GI scores (under 55).

**Hydrochloric acid**
Hydrochloric acid, or stomach acid, is the acid component of gastric juice. It plays a number of important roles in the process of digestion, including creating the right acidic environment for protein digestion to occur and killing many pathogens present in food.

**Insulin**
The hormone insulin is produced by the pancreas and helps glucose to enter the body's cells where it is used up as fuel. Insulin is also a storage hormone in that it will cause any excess glucose that is not needed immediately for energy to be stored as glycogen in the liver or muscles, or converted to fat and stored in body tissue.

**Insulin threshold**
The point at which the level of glucose in the body rises so high that it tips insulin production over optimum levels, thus encouraging glucose to be added to the body's fat stores.

**Insulin trigger**
Factor that encourages glucose levels to rise, such as foods easily converted into glucose, but also caffeine, smoking and stress.

**Irritable bowel syndrome (IBS)**
Irritable bowel syndrome, also known as spastic colon, is a common disorder whereby the regular waves of muscular movement along the intestines become uncoordinated. This disruption, involving both the small intestine and the colon, results in a variety of

symptoms in all areas of the digestive tract, including intermittent diarrhoea and constipation, cramp-like abdominal pain and swelling of the abdomen.

## Metabolic rate
The energy required to keep the body functioning while at rest.

## Metabolism
The "burning" of glucose in body cells to produce energy.

## Minerals
Substances, such as calcium, magnesium and iron, that are naturally found in various foods and which are required by the body for the maintenance of good health. A balanced, healthy diet usually contains all the minerals the body requires.

## Nutrients
Vital substances required by all living organisms for survival.

## Organic produce
Food that has been produced using farming methods that severely restrict the use of artificial chemical fertilizers and pesticides, and animals reared without the routine use of the drugs, antibiotics and wormers common in non-organic intensive livestock farming. Any organic product sold in the UK must, by law, display a certification symbol or number: the Soil Association's organic symbol is the UK's official certification mark.

## Osteoporosis
A condition in which the density of bones declines, making them brittle and prone to fracture. The mineral calcium is essential for bone health.

## Protein
A complex compound, made of carbon, hydrogen, oxygen and nitrogen and often sulphur, which is essential to all living things. Protein is required for growth and repair and is broken down into amino acids by the body.

## Saliva
An alkaline liquid secreted by the salivary glands into the mouth. Saliva lubricates food, which helps with the process of chewing and swallowing, and contains an enzyme that helps to break down the starch contained in foods. It also has antibacterial properties.

## Saturated fats
Saturated fats are primarily animal fats that are solid at room temperature. They are found in meat and dairy produce. Coconut oil is the only vegetable oil that contains a significant amount of saturated fats. Saturated fats have been shown to raise the levels of "bad" low-density lipoprotein (LDL) cholesterol in the blood.

## Set point
The point at which the body's intake of food provides exactly the amount of glucose required for its day-to-day energy requirements.

## Simple carbohydrate
A food that yields simple sugars, which are broken down rapidly into glucose by the body.

## Stimulants
Substances, including caffeine, found in foods and drinks, such as chocolate and fizzy drinks, that stimulate the production of adrenaline from the adrenal glands. Under normal circumstances, this release of adrenaline prepares the body for the "flight or fight" response syndrome, causing – among many things – the heart to beat faster (see p.20). If adrenaline is overproduced because stimulant foods have been consumed, this may lead to fatigue and blood-glucose imbalances in the body.

## Type 2 diabetes
*Diabetes mellitus* is a condition in which blood-glucose levels can become dangerously high because the body cannot utilize glucose properly. Excess blood-glucose levels (hyperglycaemia)

can result in long-term damage to the eyes, kidneys, nerves, heart and major arteries. There are two principal types of diabetes: insulin-dependent Type 1 diabetes, and non-insulin dependent Type 2 diabetes, also known as adult-onset diabetes.

In Type 2 diabetes the body is unable make enough insulin, or the body's cell receptors do not respond to insulin (this is also known as insulin resistance). This type of diabetes usually occurs in people over the age of 40, although it is becoming increasingly common in the younger population due to an increase in high-sugar, refined carbohydrate diets – even teenagers are now being diagnosed.

## Vitamins
Groups of complex organic substances, found in many different foods, that are essential in small amounts for the normal functioning of the body. There are 13 vitamins, and with the exception of vitamin D and niacin, which can be generated by the body, vitamins must be obtained from your diet. A varied diet will contain adequate amounts of all the vitamins.

## Yeast
A single cell organism used in some food industry processes such as baking, brewing and winemaking. Some yeasts naturally occur in the body, for example, for example, *Candida albicans*, which causes thrush. It is normally kept in check by "friendly" bacteria, but excess sugar, alcohol, stress and antibiotics can cause it to proliferate, resulting in oral or vaginal thrush.

# Useful addresses and websites

*Please note that, because of the fast-changing nature of the worldwide web, some websites may be out of date by the time you read this.*

## ORGANISATIONS IN THE UK AND THE REPUBLIC OF IRELAND

### The Food Doctor
76–78 Holland Park Avenue
London W11 3RB
tel: 0800 093 5877
www.thefooddoctor.com

You can also sign up to my website at **www.dk.com/fooddoctortips** to receive a monthly email full of encouragement.

### BCNH – UK College of Nutrition and Health
PO Box 43807
London NW6 3WQ
tel: 0207 372 5740
www.bcnh.co.uk

### Institute of Optimum Nutrition
13 Blades Court, Deodar Road
Putney, London SW15 2NU
tel: 0208 877 9993
www.ion.ac.uk

### Soil Association
Bristol House
40–56 Victoria Street
Bristol BS1 6BY
tel: 0117 929 0661
www.soilassociation.org
Campaigning and certification
organisation for organic food
and farming.

### www.gymguide.co.uk
Directory of health, fitness, sports and
leisure clubs in the UK.

*For information on specific digestive or other health disorders you may find the following contact details helpful.*

### Allergy UK
3 White Oak Square
London Road
Swanley
Kent BR8 7AG
allergy helpline tel: 01322 619864
www.allergyfoundation.com

### British Heart Foundation
14 Fitzhardinge Street
London W1H 6DH
helpline tel: 08450 708070
www.bhf.org.uk

### Coeliac Society of Ireland
Carmichael House
4 North Brunswick Street
Dublin 7
Ireland
tel: (01) 872 1471
www.coeliac@iol.ie

### Coeliac UK
PO Box 220
High Wycombe
Bucks HP11 2HY
helpline tel: 0870 444 8804
www.coeliac.co.uk
Charity supporting people with gluten
intolerance.

### CORE
3 St Andrews Place
London NW1 4LB
tel: 0207 486 0341
www.corecharity.org.uk
CORE is the new name for the
Digestive Disorders Foundation.

### Diabetes Federation of Ireland
76 Lower Gardiner Street
Dublin 1
tel: (01) 836 3022
helpline tel: 1 850 909 909
www.diabetes.ie

### Heart UK
7 North Road
Maidenhead
Berkshire SL6 1PE
tel: 01628 628638
www.heartuk.org.uk
Supports and advises anyone wishing
to reduce the risks of heart disease.

### The IBS Network
Northern General Hospital
Sheffield S5 7AU
www.ibsnetwork.org.uk
For enquiries relating to gut reaction
and IBS Network publications.

### Irish Heart Foundation
4 Clyde Road
Ballsbridge
Dublin 4
tel: (01) 668 5001
www.irishheart.ie

### Irish Nutrition and Dietetic Institute
Ashgrove House
Kill Avenue
Dun Laoghaire
Co. Dublin
info@indie.ie

### www.lactose.co.uk
Information on lactose intolerance,
milk allergies and IBS.

National Association for Colitis
and Crohn's Disease
4 Beaumont House
Sutton Road, St Albans
Herts AL1 5HH
tel: 0845 130 2233
www.nacc.org.uk

National Osteoporosis Society
Camerton
Bath BA2 OPJ
tel: 01761 471771
www.nos.org.uk

## ORGANISATIONS IN AUSTRALIA

### Allergy, Sensitivity and Environmental Health Association
PO Box 96
Margate
QLD 4019
tel: 07 3284 8742
www.asehaqld.org.au

### Australian Crohn's and Colitis Association
PO Box 207
13/96 Manchester Rd
Moroolbark
VIC 3138
tel: 03 9726 9008
www.acca.net.au
Provides helpful information and links
about colitis and Crohn's disease.

### Blackmores
23 Roseberry St
Balgowlah
NSW 2093
Advisory service tel: 1800 803 760
www.blackmores.com.au
Website has online health experts and
advice about numerous dietary
problems and herbal supplements.

Coeliac Society of Australia
Unit 1
306 Victoria Ave
Chatswood
NSW 2067
tel: 02 9411 4100
www.coeliac.org.au

Diabetes Australia
GPO Box 3156
Canberra
ACT 2601
tel: 1300 136 588
www.diabetesaustralia.com.au

www.foodwatch.com.au
Comprehensive website about nutrition
and diet.

www.gastro.net.au
Authoritative resource in
gastroenterology – online information
service for patients and health
professionals written by experienced
gastroenterologists.

### Gut Foundation
c/o Gastrointestinal Unit
The Prince of Wales Hospital
Randwick
NSW 2031
tel: 02 9382 2789
www.gut.nsw.edu.au

### Irritable Bowel Information and Support Association of Australia
PO Box 5044
Manly
QLD 4179
tel: 07 3893 1131
www.ibis-australia.org.au

Nutrition Australia (Victoria)
c/o Caulfield General Medical
Centre
260 Kooyong Rd
Caulfield
VIC 3162
tel: 03 9528 2453
www.nutritionaustralia.org

# Index

# About the author

**Ian Marber**
MBANT Dip ION

Nutrition consultant, author, broadcaster and health journalist

Ian studied at London's renowned Institute for Optimum Nutrition, and now heads The Food Doctor clinic at Notting Hill, London. He contributes regularly to many of Britain's leading magazines and newspapers, including *Marie Claire*, *Eve*, *Attitude*, *The Times*, *Evening Standard* and *ES*. In addition, he is an advisor and contributing editor for *Healthy* and *Here's Health*, two of Britain's most influential health magazines. Ian is also a sought-after guest on national television, appearing regularly on the BBC, Channel 4, ITN News and GMTV, as well as on many radio shows. He has also made a 15-part series for the Discovery Health channel.

Undiagnosed food sensitivities in his twenties led to Ian becoming interested in nutrition. His condition was later identified as coeliac disease, a life-long intolerance to gluten. He is now an acknowledged expert on nutrition and digestion, and many of his clients are referred to his clinic by doctors and gastroenterologists.

Ian advises on all aspects of nutrition, and in particular on the impact that correct food choices can have on health. He is known by his clients to give highly motivational, positive and practical advice that can make a real difference to their well-being.

His first book, *The Food Doctor – Healing Foods for Mind and Body*, was co-written with Vicki Edgson, in 1999. To date, it has sold around 500,000 copies and has been translated into nine languages. Ian's first solo title, *The Food Doctor in the City*, published in 2000, highlighted how to stay healthy in an urban environment. It was followed in 2001 by *In Bed with The Food Doctor*, which examines how nutrition can improve your libido and help you sleep well.

In 2003 his book *The Food Doctor Diet* became an instant bestseller. Tested on Channel 4's *Richard and Judy* by three volunteers, who each lost a dress size in only three weeks, *The Food Doctor Diet* has been hailed as a truly sensible, healthy approach to weight loss that actually works in both the long and short term.

## Acknowledgements

Thanks to all at DK for their enthusiasm, support and food, especially MC, Stephanie, Jenny, Catherine, Hermione and Antonia.

Heartfelt thanks to my dear family and wonderful friends and also to everyone at The Food Doctor. Special thanks to everyone who took the time to contact me with their success stories having read and adopted the principles in *The Food Doctor Diet*.

The publisher would like to thank Zoe Moore for editorial assistance and Hilary Bird for the index.

## About The Food Doctor

Ian Marber and Vicki Edgson co-founded their Food Doctor nutrition practice in 1999 following the success of their original book, *The Food Doctor – Healing Foods for Mind and Body*.

The consultancy is now a leading provider of nutritional information and services, including a busy clinic in West London and a network of nutrition consultants operating throughout the UK. The Food Doctor offers one-to-one consultations, workshops and lectures on a wide variety of subjects such as

weight loss, children's nutrition, digestive health and stress management. It also works with major corporate clients to improve the health and well-being of their employees and is frequently asked to work with professional caterers to ensure a healthy choice of food is available.

The Food Doctor has developed its own food range to provide healthy meal solutions and snacks: all of these are designed to incorporate The Food Doctor ethos of balance and correct nutrition.